Con

**SOWING THE SEEDS FOR CHANGE IN
BUSINESS LEADERSHIP**

Esther Walker

Co-written with the Universe

Published by Forward
Thinking Publishing

First published 2021

Published by Forward Thinking Publishing

The information given in this book should not be treated as a substitute for professional medical advice; always consult a medical practitioner. Any use of information in this book is at the reader's discretion and risk. Neither the author nor the publisher can be held responsible for any loss, claim or damage arising out of the use, or misuse, of the suggestions made, the failure to take medical advice or for any material on third party websites.

A catalogue record for this book is available from the British Library.

ISBN: 978-1-8380445-7-2

Contents

Introduction

DO YOU FEEL AT dis-ease with the way you are living, working, *BEING*? Do you feel like you are striving and not thriving in your life and business leadership? The current workplace culture that I have experienced, often places people and their potential into dis-ease. This is because profit is the primary focus and there is little consideration for the concepts of change that I am going to share with you in this book.

In many of the workplace and leadership concepts and structures today there is a loss of individual potentiality through the loss of being able to relate to our own Self and to others. It has created a disease that creates pain, it is a corporate and company curse that comes from fear:

- a fear from the loss of identification and connection with our true Self
- a fear to be authentic, in our sense of Self and in our leadership
- a fear to question the definitions of the concepts of the systems and structures within the workplace that do not fit with our own values, ethics, or morals
- a fear to stand out and stand up and be different

When fear is prevalent it becomes conflictual, there is a lack of clarity, there is conflict, there is crisis, there is challenge and when this is in the workforce, pain is also prevalent. When there is limited health in the workplace it breeds a culture of dis-ease, and this disease becomes a prominent dynamic.

Through my own very painful experiences in the workplace, I became aware of an inner knowing of what was acceptable in this environment, of what was ethical and what was unacceptable, unethical, unfair, and even inhumane. I see now that I was largely unconscious in my leadership. But there was a pivotal point during my journey where I ignited the real identification with the Self, the true spirit of me that brought me to consider concepts for change. Through my own identification - a process which I will share with you in Chapter 1, I became more conscious, more awake, and this led me to consider a new way of leadership.

It is this new dimensional mode of conscious leadership that I wish to share with you, for your own consideration, because I know I am not alone with these painful experiences of the workplace and of leadership. I know that many others feel the dis-ease I felt, but it does not have to be this way.

Through these considerations for change you can eliminate the pain and the fear, and you can move from a place of pain to one of gain. When you eliminate the pain of being at dis-ease, of feeling stressed, unhappy, unfulfilled, in conflict or even in crisis, either with your Self or the Company, when you alleviate that, you elevate the person. It is this elevation of the human spirit, through the elevation of the emotion and the elevation of the mind, that allows the creation of aspiration, innovation, and inspiration to be ignited.

I ask you to *consider,* by reading this book, your own elevation, your own emergence into your true potential as this is all possible for you through the ability to relate firstly to the Self, secondly to the Company and then to a wider workforce in your leadership. If you feel different in your leadership and want to create a difference in these changing times, this book will enable you to consider and create the changes needed.

In today's modern society we know little of ourselves and who we are. We often know nothing about our why, our purpose - which is our special reason for being here in the world. If there is an inability to relate to your own being, you cannot come into a new way of life or leadership.

It is from deeply knowing yourself, from being aware and in touch with your own passions, your values, your beliefs and your why, that enables you to live a joyful and purposeful life. There is a proven link that we live longer lives when we feel clear on what we are here to do.

By connecting to your own being, your own sense of Self, you can achieve massive transformation and I believe these are transformative times we are living in. Many more of us are being called forward into a heightened conscious awareness which shows that how we were living before the Covid-19 global pandemic does not serve us and is no longer wanted. There is a rising consciousness, and in these uncertain times, it is creating dissatisfaction. People will want more. You can already see this now in the people and their behaviour. Dissatisfaction is everywhere. People are beginning to complain. Why? I believe they are becoming conscious that they deserve more, that they desire to belong, to connect, to be treated equally, fairly, and to be thought about. Humanity is rising, and it is evident. Don't you think?

Over recent months there have been several articles that have caught my attention on social media platforms or debates on the news, where people have expressed the common theme of desiring change in the workplace. I have read the personal stories that people have openly shared as a result of losing their jobs during this pandemic. Where people in senior leadership positions with the titles to reflect their importance (that our society norms associate with personal success and something to aspire to), have found personal fulfilment far from where they were seeking it. Stories about swapping the boardroom to become a delivery driver for a supermarket chain with a vastly reduced salary but a hugely increased sense of personal fulfilment. This is achieved largely through connection with others, which creates a personal sense of doing good for others, of making a difference to others, of community and connection. As more people have experienced a new way of being, people are finding their voice. It feels like a collective light bulb has been switched on as people realise there is another way. A shared sense of unity, a human connection that is much needed in the work-place.

The lockdown and periods of being fur-loughed from work have also enabled a stillness and space that many have used for personal re-flection. Time spent at home with family and loved ones has enabled a focus upon what is re-ally valued in life, our health is under threat - a realisation that life is to be cherished! We can clearly see the lack of time for human connec-tion with others and with oneself, family time, relaxation and participation in those activities that bring you joy. There has been an apparent recognition that for many our place of work is not a positive life experience. Many feel under-valued, under recognised, under rewarded, and unfulfilled; even for those with the compensa-tion of a large salary. A relentless sense of never being 'on top of it' or in control of the volume of deadlines, emails and demands despite working all hours, of life passing by at lightning speed. Working within structures where there is a 'flow and let go' culture where you can be easily re-placed, it is fear-based. We live in a world where mental health related illness and suicide rates are increasing, achieving personal success at the cost of others is the norm, where mistakes are often viewed as shortcomings and failings rather than opportunities for growth and learning.

You do not need my words, you can see what is out there already, you can see how the unacceptable has become acceptable. This approach, where people are treated unfairly, can only lead to further difficulties in employment, employees, and companies, where the fear-based striving, struggle, and stress to survive is on the cusp. It is part of the pain of change, for through this there will be a further demand for change. We are already seeing a growing youth of creative and nonconformist talent creating finance and businesses online, creating a wave of change where larger companies will be forced to work differently. A new generation will not want the constraints, they will not want the exploitation, the dysfunction, the entrapment, the injustice, or discrimination. The societal conditioned belief that climbing the corporate ladder is the desired destination and where the definition of success is found, is becoming outdated. Therefore, these larger companies will have to be attractive as employers, they will need to return to the old ways of honour and respect. These types of companies will need to consider their own change and to actualise into being attractive employers, aligned with all the concepts for change that I share in Chapter 11.

Many of us now do not want to return to what was 'normal' - we want a new way. Through this crisis, this period of stillness that on a Universal level has taught us to stop, reflect, listen, and look within, we are being shown everything that does not serve us. To question outdated systems and structures that create stress and exhaustion, the dis-ease I refer to.

The Time is Now

It is time to create the changes necessary so that we can live more joyful and purposeful lives, being of service to each other. We are all being called to stand up and stand out, to heal past wounds by looking deep within and connecting and coming into awareness with who we are and what we are here to do. We want to become authentic and be visible and confident in who we are. More people are seeking their purpose and wanting to create successful careers aligned to their own concepts and values.

There is a calling to a more feminine way of living, working and being, particularly within leadership. There is little of the feminine in the systems and structures that lead or serve us today and we are being called to lead more from the heart and soul, with a focus on people first and foremost. A compassionate and considerate approach is needed that considers people and planet. There is a need to return to ancient ways of living and leadership where people knew the art of being in life and business, where there was a deep connection to each other and to nature.

For your understanding when I refer to the feminine, I am referring to the qualities and attributes that the feminine represents. There is a Universal energy (unity consciousness) that makes up everything and that connects everything, we are all connected to it and to each other. Although this energy is genderless, we each have a duality to ourselves, male and female attributes that make up our persona, or yin and yang if you prefer.

In brief, and for purpose of introduction, the masculine attributes particularly of today's leadership are focused on the external and action, built upon strategic and logical thinking. The way in which we perceive power in today's culture is largely a masculine system, and this approach delivers results when an actionable plan is the way to achieve a predictable outcome. As I shared previously, these are unpredictable times and people are now yearning for more, real connection, a sense of belonging, a sense of purpose, of identifying with our highest potential to discover and actualise our unique special purpose for use in service to something larger than ourselves. The feminine way is about the pause, looking inwards, reflection, care, compassion, consideration, connecting to nature, and being in a state of flow. In life and leadership, we need both, like everything in life, balance is the desired state.

We are out of balance, within our own physical human structure and the structures that we work and live by, there is too much doing, without awareness or reflection. There is a dominant masculine energy within leadership structures and systems, which is no surprise given the disproportionately small number of women who sit in senior leadership positions. These structures and systems do not serve or support her. I do not write that as a feminist either, it is simply the truth and what I have personally experienced. It is balance that is needed.

My Motivation for this Book

Although I am essentially sharing with you my story, what I have learned from my life experiences and how I hope it may help you; this is not a self-help book for I am not presenting you with the answers to your problems. I always knew that this book would be a bit different because as the title suggests I am asking you to *consider* and to find your own answers. All that you seek is within you.

I share my story to highlight to you the pain and the pitfalls that I experienced, whilst trying to fit in with masculine, power-based definitions of leadership. Of striving for a definition of success that I had not considered for myself, because I had never considered my Self.

I want to seed the considerations for change for anyone that is struggling in their business leadership. If you feel a struggle to survive, a struggle to thrive, a struggle to succeed, a struggle to stop the stress, then I want to say to you that you can change this for yourself through considering what I share with you.

Change has its own psychology; it has its own sociology. I am asking you to consider for your own leadership a new modality of management. It is a way connected to ancient leadership and it is a way that can still have enhanced productivity and profit but not from the point of where your understanding, intellect and current perception lies. In today's structures and systems that lead and govern, productivity and profit are achieved by trampling over lives, lives that lose meaning, purpose, priority, and importance. This is no way to bring the potential out of people.

I share with you concepts for your own consideration that embrace unity consciousness, where we align humanity as a whole and where people come before profit. I would like you to consider a new structure, a new thought process, a new understanding, where leadership recognition is all about bringing forth the potential of the people and sharing the rewards for their work. For what is out there is little more than a workhouse. The rewards may be bigger but there is no more happiness, connection, or health. It is devoid of emotion and full of the material, with no depth of meaning or consciousness of under-standing what truly matters.

I have considered and reconsidered and then considered again, sharing what I am about to with you and to address the meaning of the words on the front cover, 'Co-written with the Universe'. I have considered this greatly because I realise that this may be a concept too far re-moved from the current level of consciousness to consider, and I want for the wisdom I share in these pages to be fully considered and not to be taken as being woo-woo! However, I believe that we are all on a journey to reawakening, to com-ing into a more conscious awareness of the need for change, which starts with each of us becom-ing aware of our true identity, our unique Self. This is the era of authenticity and truth. This is my truth and my experience, and these words will be considered by those who are meant to consider them. It is for me to simply offer them to you for consideration.

I have, over the past year, received chan-nelled messages, ancient wisdom based on the principles of Native American leadership and divine wisdom from the celestial realms to bring peace and balance to humanity. Interestingly, you will see that these messages are directly, related to my own experiences that I share with you, and are also very much connected to my own innate knowing about my own purpose and my why. I refer to these channellings as 'Conversations with my Soul'. As I have learned that we are all encoded at the core, not with a false, corporate, fake identify but with unique Soul DNA that holds the key for your greatness and potential that you entered this world to manifest into being. Your own art of being. These channelled messages are from my spirit to yours and I share this wisdom in service to the greater good of humanity.

Throughout this book, I am presenting to you concepts that you can use that will take your business and leadership to the next level through a different way of leadership, a greatly needed way of leadership. Concepts for consideration for change, for your own gentle consideration.

Without consideration, what I share cannot be understood, acknowledged, implemented, or integrated into one's intellect. For when you consider something, there is an instant expansion just through the sheer transformation of consideration. When you are considering, you are thinking, you have the capacity to feel and the capacity to connect, to belong, to identify and to actualise.

And so, as I present my recommendations for change to you for your own gentle consideration, I firstly ask you to consider this, when was the last time you:

stopped

paused

retreated

and

considered?

Let's begin with the first consideration I would like you to consider, *you*.

Your own true identification, the concept of your Self, your Spirit, through a process I call the Five Facets of the Self.

CHAPTER 1

Five Facets of the Self

"Your understanding of your inner Self holds the meaning of your life"

Leo Tolstoy

IT IS IN THE Self that success lies, in your ability to see who you are, what you are and where you want to go. Without understanding your Self, you do not know your why, you cannot consider your own emergence into your greatest potential in life or leadership and thereby you will limit your success. You cannot fully consider the four core concepts for change that I share in Chapter 11 if you cannot identify and stand solid in your own sense of being. Concepts that will lead to a new dimensional mode of conscious leadership.

Therefore, this is where the process of change must begin. It ALL begins with the identification of the Self, which is the spirit of you.

Before I introduce you to the Five Facets of the Self.

Let's start with the word Self. This is your spirit. It has many connotations, definitions, concepts to consider.

- What does the word mean?
- What does it mean to an individual?
- What does it mean to you?

I am not talking religion or even spirituality, I am talking about a deep connection to the pure root and core of your own creation in human form. To consider this definition is the starting point to a new dimensional mode of conscious leadership, it is for you to really reflect upon the definition for yourself to find your own true identification. You may see it as the life force within human form, or perhaps you think this as a concept is all a bit woo-woo.

Let me share what it means to me because I have given this a great deal of consideration. The first definition of Self/Spirit begins with the

uniqueness that is seldom identified, a personality, a persona, an identification.

Why is this seldom identified?

Because it is not considered important to
identify with and this is done to diminish power.
If an individual cannot identify with their inner
being, then they cannot identify with their Self,
their inner being is their Spirit. We live in a
world where it is not considered, consciously
not considered, as a form of conscious control
and there is little unique spirited identification.

Whatever definition you choose to have; personality, persona, essence, inner being, before
anything else, it is coming home to this understanding of your own uniqueness, your special
purpose for being here. For at this very beginning, if a definition cannot be acknowledged, a
true identification cannot come into place.

The second definition I ask you to consider is
that without identification of your Self, nothing
can come into being, to actualise. To actualise is
to give birth, it is to actually be it. If there is no
identification, then you cannot consciously consider change in your life or leadership, because
you have no true identification of your Self to
benchmark or align these concepts against. You
will be like I was, leading from a place of unconsciousness, trying to fit in with no awareness of

whether the concepts of the structures or systems support or diminish you. This creates the pain and dis-ease that is prevalent in the workplace.

You may be familiar with the saying 'be the change you want to see', well this is it. To create the change you seek in your life and leadership, and to move from pain to gain, you have to identify the change that is needed within you first, then actually be it. You can then consider change in the company and your leadership. It is a simple equation; Self first, business second.

To actualise is to remove your Self from what has been, remove your Self from expectations, and remove your Self from a trend of opinions and thoughts. It is allowing your Self to be, with no need for external gratification, through other people's acceptance and stereotypes. The spirit cannot be stereotyped - it is unique in its individual form. It gives to you everything. It fills your destiny and when you try to fit in you create pain, because it is not you.

As I have learned, if you know little of yourself and who you are, you know nothing about your why. If you feel disconnected from your authentic Self, this is reflected in your experience with others and how you relate to them and they to you. Not having connection with yourself can result in you completely losing track of meeting your most basic of human needs. As human beings we need to belong, we need to be treated with honour and respect and kindness and care. We need to receive unconditional love and acceptance. We need to thrive through being given a sense of Self, a priority, an importance, a potential, a purpose, and a presence. How can we thrive if we don't know who we are?

In my own search for my true identification, I considered the Five Facets of the Self that enable you to become the finder of the true Self. By considering these questions this is what you are doing, the focus is on that truth. As you focus into authentically identifying, you will dissolve the association with the false Self, the fear-based Self. In dissolving that, you will begin to truly associate with what is the spirit of your identity, the true power of the unlimited potential within you. This kind of power has been feared when it should be revered. Therefore, the entire concept of the Self has been lost and is not seen in today's system and structures of leadership. It must return to the individual in this new mode of conscious leadership.

I have asked you to consider this as the first concept for change because the change must happen within you firstly. For you to begin to identify the Self on a personal level and a professional level, it is important for you to identify where you currently are, as this is the start of the art of coming into *being*. With the Self both personally and professionally, both in life and in leadership. Often there is no separation between the two, for they are interlinked and correlate with each other. What affects one affects the other. There is a synchronicity, where, in essence, there is no personal and professional because the two are one. The person is in the profession and the profession is in the person and so this has a cause and effect on how you are being.

This is how you move to a place of conscious leadership beyond the realms of equality, where people and their potential are placed before profit. From this identification you can intellectually consider and conceptualise the concepts for change that I share in Chapter 11 and create change in your life, business, and leadership.

This is the key to living a purposeful and joyful life where all people are considered.

The Five Facets of the Self are made up of the following questions:

1. Do you know your own values and beliefs?
2. Do you know how you define success and happiness?
3. Do you know what brings you fulfilment?

4. Do you know what your priority is in life or leadership?
5. Do you know how you wish to relate to yourself and to others?

If you don't feel clear on your answers or are struggling to even think of an answer, don't worry most people don't. I certainly didn't as my story in the following chapters will show you. Let us just consider these questions for a moment.

These questions are really very important, they are kind of a big deal as I have highlighted, aren't they? They can be referred to as the Five Facets of the Self. These along with the five senses we are taught at school; to see, to hear, to smell, to taste, to touch and the sixth sense, your soul intuition (that we are not taught), are the identification of your being, your real identity.

"You have no need to travel anywhere. Journey within your Self, enter a mine of rubies and bathe in the splendour of your own Light"

Rumi

Through my own experiences I now know that my sense of fulfilment, happiness or success is not a destination outside of myself, it is within me. It is my being and so it is with you. We don't have to spend a lifetime searching for it or expecting others to be responsible for bringing it to us.

The answers are there in each of us already and can be accessed if we learn to pause, stop, and consider. Take the time and find the stillness to identify and actualise with who you are. So how do you find the answers to your own definitions?

There must be a pause to consider.

CONVERSATIONS WITH MY SOUL

In this world of stress and strain you have forgotten the power in the pause. To stop. In a world where you once lived you would have taken yourself into the hills, into the mountains, into the river, into the rocks and the canyons and allowed the voice of your spirit to speak. You would have connected to the wind, the air, the unseen and to the sun and the earth and the water.... this has been demolished, in a world that never stops or pauses for thought there is in this way a loss of Self. And so, to identify with anything, passion, or purpose, to identify with new considerations for change, means taking a pause to think and to feel the purpose and meaning of the words presented in this book. For an individual to seek the identification and actualisation of themselves is to take this pause,

*to stop. In this 24/7 fast-track world silence and still-
ness are seen as insanity and yet I say to you the way
things function is insane.*

To consider is to be considerate of what truly
ignites your sense of being, your sense of purpose. By pausing for thought, to retreat and take
time out to consider, the being within you will
naturally present the answers. The Five Facets of
the Self are where it all begins, of you actually
knowing who you are and what you are here to
do. It is through the identification of these, considering them for yourself, knowing your own
answers, that is the key to the art of being. I hope
that at the end of reading this book you will feel
inspired to have considered these questions for
yourself.

Knowing the answers to these Five Facets of
the Self is to have a sense of being that will bring
you fulfilment, satisfaction, success, sustainability, security, and serenity, not stress. When you
are connected to your sense of Self, there is no
stress, there is no struggle, no striving. You are
connected to your own concepts, there is no
conflict, and no competition. Coming into being,
activating your being is the very art of your essence, the art of your productivity, the art of
your profit which gives you a deeper sense of

Self, this is the identification of you. To be a successful leader you must be an authentic one. To lead authentically you must firstly know your Self. Only when you come into the art of being, can you lead differently and emerge in the new.

Now that you have taken some time to consider the Five Facets of the Self, I would like to share with you my story, both personally and professionally. As I have shared, what affects one, affects the other and so that you can see the level of dis-ease I experienced due to having no consideration for the Self. I hope that by sharing my story with you it may resonate with your own experiences, and you will take time to consider your Self.

PART 1

UNCONSCIOUS

CHAPTER 2

Adrift

IF YOU HAVE NO concept of your own being you will drift and are open to being battered by the rocks. You are open to going where the tide takes you with no clarity, no direction, and no navigation. You will be exposed to structures and concepts of how to live, work, lead, think, feel, and behave that do not serve the human potential, that are not aligned to your values or purpose.

This was me for many years. I learned that the tide will continue to take you to the same place until you see the lesson that is being presented to guide you back to your own being, to your own purpose. I share my story in both my personal and professional life, to highlight to you that if you live in this disconnected way, unconsciously, if you navigate through life and leadership with no awareness of the Self, no idea of your values or true purpose, it can create dis-ease in all aspects of your life. You will feel the disconnection on every level, even if you are not yet aware of why.

My experiences, as my story unfolds, high-light how disconnection of the Self can manifest as painful life experiences, which for me on my quest for success, were particularly magnified in a senior leadership role within the corporate world. Here I was exposed to predefined, very masculine, power-based structures and systems where the values, ethics, and concepts of how one must think, feel, behave and lead did not feel right. In fact, they felt wholly wrong and unjust to me. I felt forced to comply with these and be-cause I did not understand my own values or have a sense of who I was, as I had not consid-ered my own concepts for change, I ended up feeling utterly diminished and eventually bro-ken on every level. I felt like a corporate slave. Strong words I know, perhaps you can relate to them on some level? However, these are my words, and this is my truth and what I have ex-perienced to the very core of my being. The dis-ease these outdated concepts of structures and systems that govern us within the workplace, that focus on profit over people, limit the human potential because they diminish the human spirit.

As I have shared, in today's world there is no concept of the Self. Certainly, within the mainstream workplace and leadership structures it does not exist. We know little of ourselves or our why. We live and work disconnected from ourselves and with others. We are taught within societal and work structures to compete and compare ourselves to others. This creates feelings of failure or of not being good enough. We often trample over each other in our pursuit to be better than or to have more than the next person. Our culture uses masculine power-based concepts of how we attain success and happiness that are based on this continual drive for more; more goods for consumption, more personal power, more profit. There is no real consideration of the impact these concepts have upon our own mental health and wellbeing, or even so far as the very existence of the human-race or the planet. Sadly, as the global pandemic and climate crisis of these times highlight, these concepts do not serve us, and it is this approach to living that has created so much dis-ease.

We set ourselves goals such as; 'when I have reached a six-figure salary, when I own my dream car, when I live in a house like that, when I have reached a certain position', we will feel many positive emotions because that it what we are taught to expect. We focus on the goal, which is normally a material possession, money, title, position, and the notion that having more and more, somehow leads to greater fulfilment. We glamourise living busy and demanding lives, where it is seen to be something to be aspired to. We are constantly working, masters of our own distraction, never switching off and with little time for anything else, doing more and more until, like a candle burning at both ends, we burn out. As you can see from my story that is how I ended up searching for something else. I hope that by reading my story this will prevent you from doing the same.

From societal conditioning, my upbringing and schooling, I believed that success (which to me equated to earning enough money to not have to worry about it) was the goal to life and being successful was therefore my priority in life. I put that first before everything else, even deciding that another important life goal I had set for myself, motherhood, could only happen when I was 'successful' so that when the time came, I was financially comfortable. I believed that personal happiness and fulfilment were intrinsically linked to success and would magically appear in all their glory once I had reached my goal.

I was trying to achieve a goal, not because of who I was or how I felt (which I did not even know), but because my belief system was that I should strive for this. My focus was never on the journey but always on the destination. I know I am not alone in this approach to life and that you may relate to this. I know when I was living this way, I was exhausted, in the struggle to reach a destination that was a false concept.

CONVERSATIONS WITH MY SOUL

In the misplaced world we live in you have been led to believe that there is a destination, a destination that once reached, then life is perfection. You have been taught this way. And yet, as you have personally experienced, striving, struggling, stressing for a destination that is not associated with your true Self, the spirit within, did not deliver anything meaningful, whole, or fulfilled and now you know it never can.

You see, I have expert first-hand experience of the pitfalls and the pain of navigating life with no consideration of the Five Facets of the Self, no answers to these five questions that I asked you to consider in the first chapter. In fact, I had not even considered these questions until I was presented with a life changing event some eight years ago.

Turning for a moment back to the questions that form the Five Facets of the Self, specifically numbers 1 and 5, which, to recap, are: -

1. Do you know your own values and beliefs?
5. Do you know how you wish to relate to yourself and to others?

I gave these two questions absolutely zero consideration. A few years ago, if you had asked me what my values were or how did I relate to myself, I don't think I would have even understood the question. Until several spiritual experiences showed up in my life, I had zero concept of my sense of Self, my being, a sense of any deeper purpose to my life. I had no awareness.

"Awareness is transformative so before any change can happen, we've got to get to know who we are and what we are here to do"

Anna Anderson

In today's world we live completely detached from any sense of intelligence about our divine nature; we are disconnected from our own sense of Self and the universal consciousness that connects us all. Most people are off track, like I was, not following their own inner guidance system, their inner intelligence, their inner knowing. Not considering their own concepts for success, happiness, or fulfilment. Many people are trying to navigate through life and leadership with a navigation system that has been created externally to themselves. A navigation system that is built upon concepts that are based upon a profit-based definition of success, with a relentless focus upon achieving more, doing more, and having more. Outdated external concepts that are out of balance and do not serve the human spirit.

It is not in the doing that success is found, it is in the pause.

I invite you now to take a pause from considering my words and I will, in the next chapter, move to telling you a little of my personal story to highlight how the disconnection from my Self manifested in painful experiences in all aspects of my life. How off track I was, setting off towards a destination of success unconsciously, with no consideration of the Five Facets of the Self, and struggling and striving within masculine power-based structures that did not support me. In my personal life, this sadly presented itself as serious fertility issues and numerous pregnancy losses. In the end, and in the darkness of my own pain and sadness, it delivered to me the pause and the stop I needed to take time to consider my Self.

CHAPTER 3

A Sense of
Something Else

*"Awakening (an act or moment of becoming
suddenly aware of something, the beginning or
rousing of something)"*

English Oxford Dictionary

I HAD NEVER FOR one moment considered that I
might struggle to conceive. Despite having many
friends in my early twenties who were starting
their families at this age, I had no interest in becoming a mother myself at that time. Although I
knew I most definitely wanted a family, I felt it
would be a natural progression when, as I have
shared with you, I had reached my goal of 'success'.

33

When I was thirty-four years old, I got married in the May of 2007. My husband and I decided that we wanted to start our family pretty much straightaway, having been together for some six years prior to tying the knot. To our delight I fell pregnant in the September. However, around seven weeks into the pregnancy I started to experience painful cramps, specifically on my left-hand side. I was referred to see a consultant gynaecologist who sadly informed my husband and I that I was experiencing an ectopic pregnancy. He proceeded to advise that I needed emergency surgery because it was a life-threatening condition, and sadly the pregnancy would also be terminated. It was shocking news to receive. In addition to feeling immense sadness for our loss, I was suddenly having a general anaesthetic and being told my life was in danger. Thankfully, the surgery was straight forward, and I physically recovered quite quickly. Emotionally though, the experience was rather traumatic, and I felt a deep sense of sadness and loss.

On a positive note, I was told that ectopic pregnancies are extremely rare and there was a very slim chance of it ever happening to me again. So, with that, we had hope and I did not ever expect this experience to be the start of what was to follow.

In May, the following year I conceived again; sheer delight and happiness, this was it! We had struggled emotionally since our first loss as our siblings had started to try for families and both my husband's brother and my sister had, shortly after our first loss, announced their wonderful news.

I was booked in for an early pregnancy scan because of what had happened before, but we were reassured by the medical professionals that it really was just a routine precaution. There was no reason to expect another ectopic. To our utter dismay and heartbreak, we were informed it was ectopic again. This time, further bad news, it was on the opposite side, my right-hand fallopian tube. Surgery followed immediately to remove the pregnancy and, unfortunately, this time the tube itself was damaged, so this was also re-moved, drastically reducing our chances of now ever conceiving naturally. We were advised that IVF was really the only hope we had and given my age, we ought to get on with it.

At the same time, in my professional life I was climbing the corporate ladder. I had accepted an offer of a role at one of the world's largest global corporations. The opportunity for a progressive, well-paid career with global travel was amazing, it ticked all the boxes that I had defined for my-self as being successful. At the time, it was also a welcome distraction to the lack of success I was experiencing in my personal life, and I threw myself into my career. I was determined to succeed in what was largely 'a man's world', struggling and striving to fit in, to meet the definitions of the concepts that defined a senior leader. Giving my all - quite literally, my time, all of it, there was no concept of work/life balance at this level of position within the hierarchical ranks. Particularly not (as I have awareness of now), for someone like me who had no consideration of herself, no concepts of what supported or diminished me. I absorbed the culture and the conditioning. I suffered health wise, due to the stress and the demands placed upon me. I see now, the stress was largely from the pressure to conform to concepts that did not support me, which I will share in the following chapters. I never switched off, and with my drive and ambition I was super-efficient and highly successful. At this time, I fast tracked my way through the company with every award for service and financial bonuses for recognition and delivery being awarded to me.

We continued with IVF for five treatments, for a further five years.

During this journey to motherhood, I became aware of a duality to myself. Let me explain what I mean by this. Firstly, there was my very controlled, efficient, logical, structured, organised, Self – my professional corporate persona, the one that I identified wholly with. I now understand this was my 'false Self' because this part of my Self had absorbed a very masculine way of thinking, feeling, and doing, to reach the corporate definition of success as a senior leader. With these masculine attributes I was successful in managing a highly complex set of operational business processes to deliver a global service. However, this wasn't me. This overriding masculine identity that I struggled and strived to adopt which I will expand upon further in the next chapter.

Secondly, there was my true Self who became very much present and in the driving seat, during this extremely painful and difficult journey to motherhood, in my personal life. What do I mean by this? There was a strong, overriding intuitive part of myself that took over, this part of my Self was very open to explore an alternative and non-logical, perhaps spiritual route even, to motherhood. I think that there was an awareness somewhere within me that as there was no certain outcome to this journey, a different approach was needed, if I was going to be successful. This more intuitive, deeper connection to an unexplained but innate knowing, that I would at some point become a mother, enabled me to consider a different path. A path that really was presented to me through a sequence of events that I realised part way along, were more than purely coincidence. There was an innate knowing, a huge well of strength within me that I had not identified with before and I felt a connection to an unseen, invisible force guiding and supporting me, the Universe as I like to refer to this now. I would just like to share a few of these experiences so you can relate to what I am sharing with you, as you may also have experienced this sort of connection.

After the first failed IVF attempt, I was looking for a hairdresser and a friend of mine recommended a salon. I went along for my appointment and immediately connected with the hairdresser. She was chatting away and suddenly said to me, "Are you trying for a baby?" I cautiously said, "Yes", wondering if I had mentioned something on the phone when I had booked the appointment and just couldn't remember. Although, why would I? She replied, "I have this really strong feeling you will have a boy." She went on to explain that she often had psychic visions and told me about a lady who was local to where I lived, called Carol, who was a spiritual healer and that I should try a healing session with her. She provided me with Carol's details and off I went oddly feeling as though I should most definitely make an appointment.

About a week later, I paid a visit to Carol. She was a wonderful welcoming person with an infectious energy and a lovely kind and caring nature. She briefly explained to me that she 'just' acted as a channel for a spirit doctor that worked through her and that she had had this gift since childhood, like it was no big deal. Whilst I was lying on her couch trying to relax with her hands moving through the air rather erratically all around me, I started to feel a tugging sensation in the region of my fallopian tube, almost like a procedure was being performed but without the excruciating pain or any hands being placed upon my body. I was slightly unnerved but believed that only good could come from this healing. Shortly after these sensations, I felt freezing cold air blowing around me, like I was suddenly sat beneath an air con unit on full blast. Carol had talked to me throughout the entire session, and I do recall feeling a bit exhausted and thinking how much I'd really like to just close my eyes for a moment and be quiet in my thoughts. Suddenly, she said to me, "I'm just going to stop talking for a moment." I closed my eyes and worried that perhaps she possessed further special powers and was also a mind reader. After about a minute had passed by, she said, "I've got your grandpa here, no sorry he says he is your Great Grandpa – Jack Elliott. He says you are to stop worrying you are going to have a son."

I could not believe my ears! The accuracy of who she said was with her, she then explained and told me that this happened from time to time during a healing, she will channel a message. She told me how she suddenly saw a rather debonaire gentleman (a fitting description from my Great Grandpa's younger years). He was asking her to be quiet as he wanted to say something. He then delivered his message and she told me she had seen him holding the baby in his arms.

Shortly after this experience, I was accompanying my Mum to a crystal healing fair that she had wanted to attend. As we were wandering around looking at the various stalls, I picked up a crystal that I thought looked interesting and just as I was about to put it back down, the stallholder said to me, "I hope you don't mind me asking, but are you trying for a baby?" I felt rather uncomfortable being asked such a direct question in public, but mumbled that, "Yes, I am" She exclaimed, "Oh how wonderful you will be having a boy."

I visited Carol on another occasion when she told me she had a lady in spirit form called Lilian, known as Lily with her and did I know anyone by this name. I couldn't think of anyone and despite everything I had experienced, I still felt rather sceptical, so asked Carol to ask how she knew me, not really expecting a reply. She came back immediately with the words "through your father Michael." My dad confirmed that he had an aunt Lilian, who they called Lily, who was my great grandpa's sister-in-law. The message that Lily had for me was "Go to the Rope Walk" repeating the words "Rope Walk" to Carol, which meant nothing to me or any of my family at the time.

About a month later, a friend I was talking to suggested that I consider trying reflexology as a natural complementary therapy to help with my ongoing fertility problems. She rooted about in her purse and handed me the reflexologist's card. I politely took it from her and glanced down at the card and saw that the address of the clinic was in Nottingham, a city I had never been to before and the building was located on the Rope Walk! The meaning of the message from Lily immediately made sense. I made an appointment at the clinic on the Rope Walk and when I met the reflexologist, without any prompting from me, he told me that he was also a spiritual healer and he felt that is what I needed, not reflexology. I smiled and relaxed and paid for the healing session.

Throughout this period of my life, I would walk, almost daily, with my dog along a local river, through fields next to my house which led to a private and beautiful pebble and, in patches, sandy beach. It was during these walks where I would release all my pent-up emotions, often screaming out loud knowing I would not be heard, allowing all the pain, sense of loss, grief, and sadness from the failed IVF cycles to release. I am sharing this very personal account with you because it was during some of these moments that I would suddenly find myself being engulfed by this immense feeling of stillness, of serenity even. This almost blissful, joyful emotion would rise-up within me and my tears of anguish would turn to tears of pure joy. It was completely and utterly strange. I could not understand or fathom where this was coming from. I now know from practicing meditation from time to time, that I was connecting with my Soul, because I can often experience this state of serenity. Have you ever felt this way?

In curiosity, and sometimes a sense of utter wonder, I wanted to seek an explanation to these rather surreal experiences and so I started to read a number of more spiritual based books. Although in this book I ask you to consider your Self, through consideration of the Five Facets of the Self so that you can find your true identity, it may also be helpful to share with you what else I have considered and learned, as I have sought to find my own true identification. Through reading other spiritual teacher's wisdom and views I started to consider that there are different aspects to a person, and as I learned these are commonly referred to as the Ego, the Inner Child, and the Self.

Let's consider these more deeply.

The Ego

I first came across the ego concept several years ago after reading Eckart Tolle 'The Power of Now' which completely resonated and made the utmost sense to me. This was a pivotal moment in the process of working towards my own identification. It presented the concept of the ego, the inner child, and the Self to me for my consideration.

Eckhart presented the concept that by living aligned with the present moment, you align your will with the Universal will, which you could call the will of God (if you are so inclined) or Source or the Universe. You do not have a separate will. The separate will is concerned with the *me*, this is the ego. But there is also a divine consciousness, the Self. There is an evolutionary impulse, and what we are doing here, at every moment, is to align ourselves with that.

My ego, that separated me from being in alignment with my Self, has an ongoing narrative built up over many years of conditioning and life experiences (including past lives and ancestral patterns if you can possibly consider that). From the age of around thirteen, when it first started to converse, to the age of forty it has sounded a lot like this:

- You are not worthy enough.
- You are not clever enough.
- You are not good enough.
- You have nothing of any use to say or give.
- You have no creative talents.
- Why are you different?
- Why can't you be more like those 'successful' leaders?
- Why can't you just fit in?
- You are pointless.

What is your ego telling you? Is it similar? I know that for many, women in particular, the narrative is similar. This is why there are so many books written about the 'imposter syndrome', a recognised condition for many women in positions of leadership who think they are not good enough for or deserving of these largely male dominated positions. I have learned that the fear of not fitting in, of not being good enough, of not deserving, are part of the collective pain of the history of women. Further to my own consideration, I believe it is because the systems and structures do not support her which makes her feel and become unauthentic, and that is what creates the imposter feelings.

As I have now considered and concluded for myself, it is not for the woman to change by disconnecting with their own feminine attributes and power as many are taught. Through learning stress management techniques and survival tools as many courses teach, or to learn to survive in these masculine power-based structures. It is for the Five Facets of the Self and the considerations of change that I share in Chapter 11 to be considered, and for people in leadership to create change. This is the way that leadership can be brought into balance and there is no need for women, in this instance, to struggle and strive or indeed for anyone regardless of gender, age, race, creed, or colour, to experience the negative emotions of the 'imposter syndrome'.

From reading Eckhart Tolle's book and many more relating to the ego, I have learned that the ego is a defence mechanism that acts in whatever negative way it needs to, to prevent you from going inwards to heal your inner child. It is an imposter, and it is not who you are. Its purpose is to keep you separated from healing your inner child and becoming an integrated and whole Self. It stops you from connecting with divine consciousness as described by Eckart Tolle. I realised that because I had many subconscious inner child wounds and had lived a life with no consideration of the Five Facets of the Self, that I had been completely at the mercy of my ego for many years.

I now see that through repeated patterns of negative life experiences, I fell into being a victim over, and over again. An interesting observation of my own ego's behaviour is the great lengths it has gone to, to prevent me from connecting with any other parts of my Self. During earlier painful experiences of my life, largely being subjected to a great deal of verbal and physical bullying as I transitioned from childhood into adulthood, my ego had always pointed the finger of blame externally at someone else, the perpetrator of my pain and not myself. It was their fault I was damaged and in so much pain and therefore with a somewhat warped logic that only that person could rescue me, I thought I must do everything I could to make that person like me. At whatever cost and always to the further diminishment of my Self, I would go back for more of the same upsetting treatment allowing others to trample all over me. I could not say no, or I would diminish myself and dim that part of me that I felt was the cause of their abuse to me, or I would hide away. I had not considered my own boundaries and how I wished to relate to myself and others to me. I know now that the other person(s) involved in these, often traumatic, experiences with their own unconscious wounds, could never heal me.

I have learned that the more unresolved wounds you have the more active your ego is, and the more you will attract all the things you work so hard to protect yourself from. I have lost count of how many times I have despaired as I realised that once again, I have been mistreated. I have had my boundaries trampled on, or I have been bullied or deeply hurt by a person I thought was a friend. I have blamed everything outside of myself. I have closed myself down and disconnected so much from life, at times from my own sense of Self, as a way to escape my inner wounds with the painful defences of self-loathing, self-abuse, fear, shame, and blame. I have tried to manage the pain, without even being aware of the cause of it. I was so entrenched in my ego that my inner child was left unattended to for many years. Therefore, I regularly self-medicated with too much alcohol, a poor diet, and other self-abusive behaviours. When my pain reached fever pitch having been stripped bare of any sense of self-worth and self-esteem in the corporate world, that I was barely surviving in, I was regularly taking prescribed beta-blockers. I used these to suppress the overriding fear and anxiety in circumstances where I knew these awful triggers would manifest.

I have learned that when you feel triggered to feel and act in a way that you know does not serve you, when your thoughts are unkind and reflect painful limiting self-beliefs, or you start to appoint blame to others for how terrible you feel about yourself, it is your ego at play here. Take the time to pause and stop and bring awareness to your thoughts. Awareness means coming into consciousness, to awaken so, just in the act of awareness, you can create change. You can consider how to release or reprogramme these thoughts and feelings that do not serve you. In the pause you can seek the answers to your pain, simply by considering what is it that the ego, through its painful narrative, is preventing you from identifying? Consider where does this limiting belief that the ego is going to great lengths to keep me from identifying come from? What is this pain that creates these self-destructive behaviours? You have to dig deep to find the root cause of the pain. You have to feel, not just to heal but to truly understand and discover.

The Inner Child

I have learned, through my own process of digging deep, that it is the inner child part of your Self that holds your subconscious wounds. These wounds create those limiting self-beliefs you may have about yourself, that your ego, if it is anything like mine, batters you with.

The more scientific concept of the inner child explains that, up to the age of around seven years old, our brain uses theta brainwaves, which do not apply reason or logic to our experiences, we also soak up every experience during these informative early years. It is also around this age that our inner programming is complete. It is not until around twelve years of age that we switch to the alpha brainwave which is the logical cognitive mind. Let's just consider this. Your inner thoughts and beliefs were established with childish emotion-based reasoning before you had the logical intelligence to accept or dismiss certain messages! When we get triggered by an event in our life this often relates to an unhealed younger part of ourselves.

To further compound this, it is at this early age that we also learn about conditional love. Through our parenting and schooling, we are taught that we are loveable and acceptable for what we did or did not do, rather than teaching us that we are wholly loveable for who we are. This means that the deep subconscious parts of our Self believe that we are unworthy unless we earn approval. This leads to the human condition for co-dependency, and now starts the belief that we need to source our worth and wholeness from outside of ourselves. We lose our sense of Self, of connection to the Universe and of unconditional love. Instead we learn that our sense of Self is connected to other people's behaviour, love, and approval. If you consider this rather deeply, you can see that the unconsciousness we see manifested in the serious challenges facing humanity today, are a direct result of a disconnect from our Self, right back to these early childhood years. We have lost the art of being, and by believing that we need to conform to definitions outside of ourselves, to all be same, to think, to feel and do the same, we become fearful to be different. The fear creates the competition and the struggle, and the stress and we disconnect from our unique creativity and unique purpose that we are here to deliver. There is limited creativity and no real change.

If as a child you did not receive the level of love and approval you sought, this creates subconscious wounds of unworthiness. We show up in the world with these young wounds forming part of our unconscious identity. If we are triggered by someone to feel unworthy, this childhood wound is activated, the unconscious then becomes conscious, and we feel pain and so the ego steps in with its stories and its painful narrative. We all have our own subconscious wounds. It could be fear of rejection which manifests in your adult life as feeling lonely. A part of the process of connecting to your true Self is to heal these wounds.

When the inner child is coming from a place of fear, self-protection, and detachment, you are disconnected from unity consciousness, from the Universe. Thus you are living in illusions of darkness and separation. In this disconnected state there is little joy, you feel unloved, unworthy, unacceptable, and unsafe and you treat yourself accordingly. You are completely controlled by your ego. If your inner child feels unsafe, unheard, damaged, rejected, or abandoned, it will scream out in pain, as I experienced, to be heard, to be helped and healed. This is what is happening when you feel those painful triggers or intense emotional anguish. If you continue to ignore the screams or have no awareness of where they are coming from, this will create disease and even sickness of the mind to get your attention. Sadly, often in today's world it can remain unheard or unhealed because the focus is on the effect not the root cause. I speak from experience; this is no way to live.

The Self

At some point during these painful experiences, particularly during my IVF years, I started to gain an insight into a different part of my Self, that could weather most storms life presented me with. A sense of there being a possibility that perhaps I could rescue my Self. I considered that if I could, even in the depths of despair, feel a sense of strength and serenity, that if I could just pause and take a moment to consider these limiting and painful thoughts, then perhaps I could change them.

As you embark on your own journey of true identification through consideration of the Five Facets of the Self. As you acknowledge your ego and the painful false things it tells you from its place of fear. As you take time to be still and listen, you will access and start to heal your inner child. We often avoid this deeper connection to ourselves because it takes courage. What do I mean by this? It is easier to listen to the ego because working through painful emotions that arise during this discovery of your Self, going into the abyss of our own shadows is, at times, very painful. But let me reassure you, that it is in the darkness that the light is found. It is this light that is transformative, it is through this process that you start to connect, to return to your Self. Now that you understand that the inner child within you formed these limiting thoughts when it was a small infant with no logical brain function, you can hopefully listen to the voice of your innocent child without judgement. In these moments of self-care, of self-healing, give it the loving space it needs to express, to be acknowledged, to be held, to be heard, with the tenderness and love you would give to any upset and lost child.

When the inner child is released in this way, you connect to the true unlimited potential of your Self. You will feel safe, protected, loved, worthy and accepted. You will feel creative, generous, loving, and joyful. You will also happily speak your truth, as you will know your answers to the Five Facets of the Self that I have asked you to consider in Chapter 1. When you know your Self, you are connected to the spirit of you. When you are connected to the spirit of you, you are connected to the Universe, living as you were always intended to live, authentically as your true magnificent Self.

This act of transformational healing is self-love and through love your ego dissolves. This is the only way to come into wholeness with one's true self, the art of being.

"The reason that ego and love are not compatible comes down to this: you cannot take your ego into the unknown, where love wants to lead. If you follow love, your life will become uncertain, and the ego craves certainty."

Deepak Chopra

Wherever you are, I invite you to take time to consider these parts of your Self and if you do not already, perhaps you could consider introducing some self-care practice into your life. Maybe try some meditation, breathwork, yoga, or spend time alone in nature. Choose whatever gives you time and space to just connect inwards and listen to your own inner child, those inner thoughts that do not serve you and hold back your own potential.

Conversations with my Soul

Having shared a little of my more unconventional journey to motherhood what I am about to share may come as no great surprise to you. In response to an inner yearning that manifested into a strong sense of calling to identify, actualise and emerge into my true purpose and potential, I was divinely presented with the path to follow.

In January 2020 I connected with Leadership and Intuitive coach, Julie Anne Hart. She provided me with a spiritual reading which I found to be so accurate in her description of my life experiences and my characteristics, that I instinctively knew I would be connecting with her again. For the past year, I have continued working with her and she has supported and guided me through her iChannel Wisdom programme. It is through working with Julie Anne that I have received the connection to my guides and received the wisdom I share with you in this book. Through this process I have re-identified with my own unique purpose, my why, for as I have learned, I am all about the why! I say 're-identified' because I have realised that my purpose has always been known to me, because it is me. You will likely experience this too when you connect with your own purpose. When you give yourself the space to consider this, it presents itself as your deepest desires, yearnings, the ones that you almost instantly dismiss because your ego falsely tells you that of course you can't do that.

We all have an innate knowing deep within, so my true Self, my spirit has never left me. I have always known my purpose, but with layers of conditioning that strip us of a sense of our Self it was lost, hidden. Rather like the story of the Golden Buddha who resided in The Temple of the Golden Buddha in Bangkok, Thailand. For years it remained, undiscovered, and hidden away under layers of protective clay to prevent it from being stolen during enemy invasion. Many years later the clay was chipped away and the beauty of the radiant gold that laid concealed underneath was revealed in all its glory. Why am I sharing this story with you? Because each of us is golden by nature. We are born knowing and connected to our true beautiful shining golden essence but then with societal and cultural conditioning we learn to think, feel and be a certain way, to conform to predefined concepts and structures that do not support the potential of the human spirit. Often as a result we learn to diminish our light, to not be so different, to fit in, and like the story we start to apply our own layers of clay, our own protective coating that hides us away and serves to keep us safe from the world. The journey to discovering your Self, is your opportunity to remove those layers of clay that weigh you down and hide your beautiful radiant light. The light of you, the light of your joyful and divine purpose.

I was living, like many are, disconnected and unconscious of my purpose, passion, feminine power, and therefore limiting my own potential and prosperity. So, what have I rediscovered about my Self and what is my why?

I am passionate about people, purpose, potential and educating others how to access their own prosperity. To teach that when you know its laws, you can become unlimited. To support others to rise into their unlimited potential in their life and leadership through a process of identification to emergence of their magnificent, real, and unique Self. Knowing yourself and being your Self is what enables you to live a purposeful and joyful life.

I am passionate about helping others in leadership positions to rise out of the dis-ease they may be experiencing, or to avoid the pain and pitfalls that I experienced by connecting to their own sense of Self, their own why, unique, and special purpose. I am also passionate about creating the change I write about and ask you in your own leadership to consider, to create a positive workplace for all, where people come before profit. This is conscious leadership.

I want to teach a new psychology in leadership through introducing change that brings balance into the leadership structures and systems that govern and shape today's world. To support women to reconnect to their feminine power and to reintroduce within the workplace the feminine attributes to leadership systems and structures that have been lost and are very much needed now.

The four core Concepts for Consideration for Change that I share in Chapter 11 are based upon the channelled wisdom and guidance that I refer to as 'Conversations with my Soul'. I also share extracts of these channelled messages throughout the next chapters where I share with you my experiences in the workplace, that as I now clearly see, have brought me to consider and teach this new way of leadership.

All that is required of you is to consider these words for your Self.

CHAPTER 4

The Pursuit of Success

My relentless pursuit and achievement of success prior to the birth of my son, served for a while as a distraction from the pain I felt due to the sadness I was experiencing in my personal life. The more I focused on anything external to myself, the less time I had to be still, to think or to feel. In moments when I could be still, I chose to numb myself with self-abusive behaviours like getting 'blind drunk' to shut off all senses. It is interesting how we often process our emotions by stuffing them back down again once they surface isn't it? Often, we are too fearful to face the reason for the pain we feel, which can result in destructive behaviours like mine at that time. I do hope that if you resonate with this that now, with awareness, you can take on board some of the concepts I shared in the previous chapter and take steps to release the emotion that does not serve you.

Despite the physically exhausting and emotionally painful journey to motherhood, in a parallel Universe I was battling my way to what I believed was success. Although, upon reflection, I realise it was not even a conscious battle because I had no understanding of myself. As I have shared, I had limited self-awareness, no consideration of the Five Facets of the Self, so no concepts, or definitions of my own.

Success had been defined for me by society. In our 24/7 fast-track world I was on the treadmill of the corporate system never pausing for thought, never considering why I felt so at disease with myself. I believe that this societal definition of success, of forever achieving more, needs to change. I now know that success is a unique definition, it is not a structured social definition defined by certain conditions or control. As I shared in the introduction, in these changing times and periods of lockdown during a global pandemic, I believe more people are becoming aware of concepts and systems and structures that define how we live and work which need to change. People do not want the conditions or the control that exploit and diminish them. On reflection, I understand that the human spirit can only be fulfilled (and by fulfilment, I mean a sense of wholeness of potential, a wholeness of purpose) through self-understanding and discovery. Therefore, success is a unique definition, it is not social. The identification of the Self is the starting process to alleviate the disease and pain that many leaders feel, like I did.

I recall a moment in 1986 at the age of 13, scratching a quote, from a poster that caught my eye on the wall in front of me, into my pencil tin with the end of my compass during a Maths lesson. The poster really resonated with me and became my life mantra. It read,

"Big shots are only little shots, that keep shooting."

I liked the idea at that young age, of being successful and all that society had led me to believe this meant. At the tender age of 21, I entered the perfect environment in pursuit of my dream of success, the corporate structure, where the emphasis was one of a relentless squeeze for more productivity and more profit. Therefore, over the years, I kept on striving to get to the top, ignoring all the warning signs from my body which, health wise, was exhausted from stress. On this corporate treadmill my focus was just to achieve more, do more, be more, have more, earn more, deliver more, to be better than, to serve the hierarchy above, and to SURVIVE.

I see, now that I am out of the environment, that you cannot have a sense of anything when you are on the treadmill of the corporate system. It strips and segregates you from your Self. Without any consideration of this, I had no awareness that it was stress and diminishment of my Self that was manifesting itself as my serious fertility issues. I was ignoring how unauthentic I had become in my focus to succeed in a tough male dominated industry, where the focus of success was purely profit driven. You may also be in this position, and I sympathise with you. It is not a great way to live. At this time, despite being repeatedly recognised for being a 'top per-former' within my leadership role, I was still be-ing asked to change. For example, I was told that in order to really make a good impression with those responsible for my career progression, I should display more masculine qualities, to shout at suppliers, to 'stop being so nice'. This was totally unauthentic behaviour for me.

I have learned that if we have no sense of our-selves, if we do not know the answers to the Five Facets of the Self, we can spend our lives just go-ing through the motions. By not identifying with who we truly are, we end up striving to meet goals not aligned to who, or what we are. This is not the route to a life of deep and meaningful purpose.

Let us just to take a moment to recap upon those Five Facets of the Self that I asked you to consider in Chapter 1. Have you considered them yet? If not, I invite you to take a pause and give them some thought now:

1. Do you know your own values and beliefs?
2. Do you know how you define success and happiness?
3. Do you know what brings you fulfilment?
4. Do you know what your priority is in life or leadership?
5. Do you know how you wish to relate to yourself and to others?

"We limit ourselves by defining ourselves"

Deepak Chopra

In today's world of profit driven purpose that strips a sense of Self and meaning, there is no sense of clarity of who we are. The clarity is in your uniqueness and the excelling of the Self through your unique gifts, skills, and purpose, your own USP. For any fellow marketeers, I do not mean a unique selling point, this is a unique sense of purpose. Your unique sense of purpose. Consider for yourself:

- What do you want to deliver that makes you happy, whole, and fulfilled?
- What is your legacy or legend?
- What do you want to be known for?

If you are feeling lost and unfulfilled, like I was, or need to seek the next level of yourself in business, you need to understand that your individual uniqueness is not found on the corporate treadmill. It is found in the power of the pause, the silence.

In the stop, there is stillness and in the stillness your answers can be found from within you. This is where success is found, in your innate knowing.

In the pause, you are pausing for this purpose, there is one simple question:-

What is it that lies unidentified about your-Self, your business role, your purpose?

CONVERSATIONS WITH MY SOUL

If you look all around you at the structures and systems that lead and govern, it is competition, it is scramble, it is climbing over another, with no consideration in the hope to get to the top or receive more. For the leader who is prepared to learn in their ability to be alone, to pause, to stop, they will seek so much more.

CHAPTER 5

Structure

As I have shared with you, eight years ago, I was working in a senior leadership position in the corporate world where title and hierarchical rank defined your sense of Self (or so I thought). I was promoted into a position with the word 'global' in the title and a job grade with a large salary and impressive annual bonuses thrown in. I thought I had reached the dizzy heights of success, only to find that when I reached this goal, it wasn't really what I was searching for after all. In fact, rather than feeling I had achieved my goals, a sense of fulfilment and all the other positive emotions one would associate with personal achievement, it had quite the opposite effect. I had moved to a large global corporate culture for what I had perceived at the time to be a marvellous opportunity for personal growth and to achieve my definition of success. I achieved the latter but failed miserably at the first. Instead of growth I experienced quite the opposite, although I learned a great deal which I will elaborate upon in the following pages.

The key lesson I learned was that if you are not connected to your Self, if you are trying to reach a goal that you have not even considered, and if you are unauthentic in your leadership, you will strive. Therefore, struggle and stress will become your normality. To reach a goal that I had been striving for, I realised what that had cost me after I had achieved it. It left me feeling panic stricken, frightened, and depressed. I felt like I had no identity at all. I did not know who I was, if I did not want this after 23 years of striving for this success, then what did I want?

I felt guilt and shame for not feeling like I was supposed to feel. My programmed beliefs were that if you are successful, climbing the corporate ladder, earning plenty of money, that you would feel happy and fulfilled. Also, as a female who had reached this level and broken through the six-figure ceiling, I felt that I should be extremely grateful for what I had. I had read Government data that reported four times more men than women in Britain earn a six-figure salary. I had pursued the definition of success that I referred to in the previous chapter and this had adversely affected my mental health and my physical health. I saw how the role and responsibilities to deliver more and more profit had consumed me so much. I had no concept of a work/life balance, nor any concept of my own health and wellbeing. It was as if a blindfold had been taken off, and in the following pages I will expand upon these experiences and the lessons that I learned.

I was deeply affected by the constraints of what I believe is an outdated concept of a corporate culture, a culture that is rife within the workplace today. A culture where the systems and structures are profit focused above all else. I strongly believe this approach simply cannot survive in these changing times - a focus on people needs to come before profit.

CONVERSATIONS WITH MY SOUL

Profit is a direct result of productivity, and it is happy and fulfilled people that create productivity. If profit is the focus of any business, this is a short-sighted vision which will result in the manipulation of the employee and cannot be sustained for the long term.

As I have highlighted in the Introduction, people want and deserve more; this approach to leadership and the workplace is creating disease.

Before I continue, I feel the need to add a personal disclaimer to state that this is not a scathing report of any previous employer or large corporation. I do not wish to name or shame, seek any personal gain nor have any agenda from sharing my experiences. I share only because I wholeheartedly wish for change to be considered and for my experiences to be eradicated. It is my understanding that there is not even any awareness or consciousness of how these systems and structures diminish people. It is seen to be a failing of the individual, the person, if they fail to fit in. This is a true, matter of fact account of what I personally experienced. Concepts of leadership within the corporate culture and structure, interspersed with my thoughts and the wisdom that has been channelled to me. I know that my experiences are shared, although to varying degrees, by many in the workplace and that there is a need for change. These structures and systems do not support the new way of leadership, the conscious leadership that I ask you to consider.

CONVERSATIONS WITH MY SOUL

Let me begin in truth, there is no consideration for whom they break in the process whether that is not paying, exploiting, using, abusing. There is no code of conduct, no ethics, and no values. None of your considerations are considered, the consideration has no consciousness. It is not even seen as needed for they have no consciousness, they know not of what they do and yet they will be forced to wake up, to see, to own and acknowledge that where they been and the path they have walked and what they are currently doing is no longer feasible, viable, sustainable. It can no longer suffice in an evolving world.

Interestingly, but not uncommonly, as more and more people are openly sharing, they are exposing this paradoxical time we find ourselves living in, where very successful people, particularly women, are more unhappy, lonely, depressed than ever before. It was at this point, where I had reached this societal definition of success, that I found myself in the darkest period of my life, almost at rock bottom. It was also the time that I was promoted to a very senior leadership position, and I recall very clearly an ex-colleague and friend saying to me,

"Esther I am delighted for you, that is an amazing accomplishment in such a short time, but you do know what they say when you get promoted to that job level don't you? They say you've sold your soul."

Never a truer word said to me. Perhaps in your professional life and leadership you feel the same?

The hierarchical leadership structure that I have experienced is one that separates. Where never the twain shall meet. Where one does not know another nor needs to. Where opportunities and payment are completely different and lines of honour, respect and value become weak at the bottom of that structure. To me, this kind of company leadership holds no understanding, no communication, because there is no sense of belonging unless you are willing to become completely conditioned by the culture, the concepts, and the definitions that do not serve all the people within that structure. This leadership does not build any kind of relationships at all.

CONVERSATIONS WITH MY SOUL

Structure is solidarity - solid, stable, secure and in today's world there is little solidarity. Solidarity is col-

lective, it is uniting, reuniting. Solid together, not sin-gular but plural.

This structure of leadership that I experienced had no solidarity, it is based on a singular structure, on an 'I am it'.

CONVERSATIONS WITH MY SOUL

A hierarchical status that has no sense of belonging or understanding, that has no broader concept, has no broader consideration, has no broader consciousness, or awareness of the interrelated dynamic of that structure. The whole structure was separated, you could partition it off into portions of segregation, the hierarchical boxes of an organisational chart that you are familiar with. I ask you to consider how does seg-regation produce solidarity? It does not - it separates.

And in that company separation it breeds stag-nation of human potential. When you have solidar-ity, you have understanding, you have knowledge, you have an awareness, you have an education, you have informed leadership, you know your people.

Often the structures and systems within the workplace are fear-based and intimating. I have, during my time in this type of corporate structure, witnessed colleagues and suppliers, both male and female, break down in tears due to stress, exhaustion, and an inability to cope with the demanding workload. It is sad for me to say, but also from bullying and manipulation. I have experienced a culture where senior leaders were to be feared and mistakes could literally mark the end for you, or so I was led to believe. I was once told prior to a meeting, with someone in such a senior position, that I should be over prepared because the person higher up the ranks liked nothing more than to 'rip you apart' and that it was like 'walking into the lion's den'. This not only bred fear and stress amongst us lower ranking employees, but it also pitted everyone against each other. It separated, as people in the team focused fearfully on their own survival by treading over another.

I have experienced a corporate culture where one must have a well-rehearsed 'elevator speech', which is a commonly understood concept in this environment, in case one should ever find oneself in the presence of such greatness as a senior leader. This implied, quite literally, that the first impression you made could determine your future with the company. I considered, 'what is wrong with just relating to another person in a non-rehearsed way, of being yourself?'

I watched my colleagues struggle with mental health and anxiety; some, like myself, were signed off work medically with stress related illnesses. Many younger females, new to the corporate environment, would reach out to me expressing their fear about presenting to senior leaders. I was told I was unlike the other people in leadership. I was approachable and a French colleague, perhaps seeking the correct English phrase, once told me I was 'the only human' in the whole of the team. I started to feel a great sense of injustice at how the structure treated people as I watched people in roles further down the hierarchical structure being disregarded.

CONVERSATIONS WITH MY SOUL

In these corporate structures most people's roles have no meaning, at the bottom there is little worth, little consideration or none and at the top there is no emotion, no meaning and so both become victim to the structure.

These structures and concepts do not serve or support the human spirit and that appears to be magnified more so than ever now that external circumstances have forced massive change to the way in which we work. Please take a moment to look around at all you see and hear about the workplace and wider context where this is evident. Company values being broken and there being no reprisal for unfair actions that hurt others or destroy lives, rendering values meaningless, diminishing trust. Senior public leaders breaking rules, out for themselves, with no apparent responsibility or accountability. People on the frontline working endless hours for little reward, barely affording to feed their families. A flow and let go approach to employment where people are treated like commodities or robots. Hierarchical structures that place leaders above and beyond and out of reach with the foundation of their business – the people. Leaders who focus on their own needs and not those of the people; where the agenda is not the people's agenda, it is an agenda grounded in a misplaced power that misuses control in the relentless pursuit of profit. The increase in work related stress and poor mental health, increasing suicide rates even.

Leadership has lost its way and the unacceptable has become acceptable.

I have given a great deal of consideration to this typical corporate structure, and I believe it needs to change. It is no longer about the top and the bottom, the above or the below but it becomes a whole, not a series of square boxes but a circle or a wheel. Every segment of that wheel is important, a consideration, a factor in the success of the whole, much akin to leadership of times past.

CONVERSATIONS WITH MY SOUL

In ancient times, it was seen to be an honour to be a leader, chosen by the Great Spirit to take responsibility for all the people's needs and that this collective need must come before their own. A leader did not have their own needs or a separate agenda, this was leadership where everybody gained.

As human beings, everybody is different. They desire different things, have different needs, and have their own dynamic and destiny. Therefore, we are not all the same. We are not all destined to be the same thing, to do the same thing, or create the same thing. Yet within that individuality, there is a commonality, a sense of belonging and fulfilment, care, respect, honour, and values to look out for each other and promote each other. I did not experience any of this in the workplace. In fact, I experienced the opposite.

CONVERSATIONS WITH MY SOUL

The definition of success has failed us in today's times. It has stripped us bare, depleted us from any kind of connection and true creation that brings happiness and true fulfilment. So much so that people have had to detach, dissociate from their senses.

I did exactly that in order to survive in that environment, and in doing so I lost a bit more of my Self. I stopped feeling, no care or compassion for my Self or for others, no sense of connection.

CONVERSATIONS WITH MY SOUL

In ancient leadership the 'why' was known. People knew their part and that part was honoured and vital as sustaining the whole. The leader was responsible in ensuring the being in the human was able to be expressed, have its needs met and promoted, where happiness prevailed.

Today's systems detach people. We cannot come together in the way of ancient leadership this channelled message speaks of, whilst we have a status, a statue of being more important and in this importance, it is only the leader that should receive, for this is not leadership.

CONVERSATIONS WITH MY SOUL

In ancient ways the leader's agenda was about the people's needs, the people's agenda, and that has now long gone. Today the structure has its own agenda, and a leader is seen to drive the people only towards achieving that corporate agenda. An agenda based upon the definition of success - more and more profit. There is no connection to the people's needs and there is no understanding of the person, of the collective power of all the people in that structure.

Leaders must connect with their own Self and place their Self in the business as a priority. For if the Self cannot survive, the people cannot survive, the service cannot survive, and the business will not survive, for the energy of the struggle is limited. It debilitates the creative spirit, it debilitates positivity, it debilitates inspiration, aspiration, and innovation until there is nothing left and the person wants out.

I can fully relate with this, and so, the leadership structure, the organisational structure that I experienced has no sense, no intellect. I look back at my own experiences in leadership and I see that because my own needs were not being met, my desire or passion were not in it and therefore, I could not excel in those opportunities. My productivity and profit became finite. Once you understand that it all starts with the Self, with you as the leader, you can build or form a more successful company or business. You will work with understanding community and connection within your company, which leads to more creation.

When a leader understands that their primary role is to promote the good of the whole organisation and place people first, they will understand that their position is out of alignment with that ethos and structure. They cannot be isolated at the top of their own castle, for they are not above, there cannot be an above or a below.

CONVERSATIONS WITH MY SOUL

Productivity is about the production of coming together to be accountable and responsible for every individual's part in the amalgamation and success of the whole. Each individual's part must be honoured and respected. The leader must understand that they are there to support, to govern and to ensure that all needs of every part are met. In essence in the circle, the wheel of a new structure, they may be in the mid-

dle of that wheel, but they are also there underneath it to lift it, to spin it, to ensure its sustainability and success.

Every role within the structure must be brought into a consideration of change. The role is an important part of the whole, the wheel, without the role there is no whole. The whole allows expansion and excellence and when the whole comes together in unity, each part being valued as in a wheel, they excel. And so, the above and the below is no longer workable, senior leaders are accountable for sustaining the welfare of their people.

I believe it is possible to still have lines of hierarchy, accountability, and roles but through a different way. There must be different lines of communication, accessible communication that can rise through each segment, but this can only happen when the leader's role is flexible and fluid on that wheel. Therefore, structure can no longer be partitioned off where 'never the twain shall meet', for when it is heavy at the top and the bottom is produced by the 'flow and let go' of people it becomes like a leaning tower, forever toppling and trying to prop itself back up. Yet these struggles, these conflicts, are seldom if you have a solid structure, based upon solid considerations, for concepts for change. If the structure remains the same then the responsibility is limited, the responsibility then becomes slightly finite, "I am responsible for this, you are responsible for that" and whilst I am not disputing boundaries in business, I am looking at what the definition of leadership means. This way of leadership can only come when the why is discovered, the leader's own why, through a consideration of the Self.

CONVERSATIONS WITH MY SOUL

And so, for the leader that is 'out to get' - then fine, that is their responsibility. But it has a cause and effect, repercussions, and reprisal. You know the cause and effect because you experienced this style of leadership, discontent, dissatisfaction, disloyalty, disorganisation, disarray, dis-ease, this is a toxic environment. The why must be explored in order to take a wider level of responsibility.

How does the structure in your company support you and all others? In the next chapter I share my thoughts based on my experiences, interspersed with the channelled wisdom I have received as we look at the topics of company culture, values and ethics.

CHAPTER 6

Culture, Values
and Ethics

WITHIN THE CORPORATE CULTURE I experienced, there was a corporate persona which was not very personable. Perhaps you recognise this in your workplace? What do I mean by this? The persona that was presented in this environment was largely devoid of emotion and an inability to relate with emotional intellect. An environment where everyone took themselves so very seriously, there was little laughter or joy. A corporate culture of one-upmanship and competition rather than support and collaboration. There was little sense of unity, although each role had its own individual goal with the same objective - to deliver more profit. In this corporate environment, I felt that I really did not fit. I was most

81

unlike my peers in my leadership style, particularly in how I related to others, how I worked with people and how I communicated with them.

I recall being asked to attend a global marketing course which contained a session on supplier management. It was being hosted by a female senior leader who felt it necessary to explain to the attendees that suppliers are human beings too, but just not so important, and that we should try to be nice to them, but not too nice. I waited for her to laugh at what surely must be a joke, a poor taste one at that, but it was meant seriously. I could see her words were being listened to intently as the largely graduate employees took notes, keen to learn the corporate way. I complained and refused to continue the course.

These were early warning signs of the misalignment with my own concepts of supplier management, which is centred upon relationship building. However, I was not conscious enough at the time to see these as warning signs. I was blindsided by my focus upon achieving success, by fitting in to this new structure, so I simply highlighted the unfairness, naively thought it would be considered and addressed and removed myself from it. As I have now considered, my own concept of supplier management and relationship building, was one based on equality of all people. I have always treated suppliers as an extension of my own team, a part of the whole, working in collaboration with mutual trust and respect, authentic relationships. There was no 'them and us', no 'I am more important'. There was a shared commitment to deliver a common goal and it did not matter to me who employed you. I was immune to corporate politics at that time, naïve perhaps, as I thought that everyone worked in this way.

I had at an earlier time in my career been given the feedback from a senior leader that I should perhaps try to be a bit more like another Account Director. When I asked for some clarification on this, the answer given was that I should have a more precalculated and strategic approach to the client relationship, to be a bit more assertive and sales focused. My manager at that time, had kindly disputed the feedback and highlighted that my relationships were authentic, they were built on trust and respect. I did not need or want to be different with any of my work relationships. Nothing more was said at that time, and I was allowed to just be myself, I believe this was because it was this client that was delivering the most profit for my employer. A relationship that I had built based on honesty, respect, working in collaboration and even having a very good time in the process – fun even, being creative together! Through reputation came recommendation, and this employer of mine went on to become the supplier of choice for this client and we gained global business as a result. Long term, high value business opportunities were gained, as opposed to the strategic 'quick wins' that I was being asked to seek via a corporate definition of 'relationship building'.

Aren't relationships just people relating to one another naturally as human beings?

Why does this need to be defined as a corporate training programme 'relationship building' where one learns techniques to manipulate an outcome like a tactical game?

I left that company because the opportunities for growth and progression were limited. Despite year on year, being promised some financial reward for our efforts, in the form of a bonus at the management level I was at, each year the company would fail to deliver, and we would experience quite the opposite, a pay freeze. Their word, year after year, clearly meant nothing. Perhaps you have experienced something similar in your workplace? It is a hugely demotivating experience, isn't it? That compromises the trust and respect between you and your employer.

I moved 'client side' as it is referred to, as a result of what I believe must have been a **recruit-**

ment policy review. There had clearly been a recognition of a need for change, for something different. The policy sought to recruit 'experienced hires' like myself, who would bring subject matter expertise instead of the normal corporate approach that often focuses solely upon the recruitment of top graduates. The best global academics would join the corporate world via a specific programme, which was extremely desirable and, from what I understood, involved a very intense and competitive recruitment process. Once hired and as per the corporate system, they are fast tracked through a company moving from one different business area to another, quickly gaining a complete overview but with little opportunity for specialism. In my experience, this was apparent to me in the volume of external contractors I worked with.

My observation from my own experience, is that the typical recruitment process is built upon a concept where profit is placed before people. There is a consideration for what type of person is needed to create a competitive edge and to deliver more profit, but there is no consideration for change in the concepts that define the systems and structure. These concepts created and deployed for graduates do not necessarily fit all types of employees. There is one box and in it you are placed, you must fit in. I bring your attention here to the adage, that 'wisdom comes with age and experience' and this, I believe, has been overlooked. This is all too often true within these structures, and so being a bit older and richer in work and life experiences, I had already experienced a different way of leadership. I had, without being aware, already defined my own leadership style, a style that was based more upon the concepts I share with you later in this book. A leadership style that delivered exceptional results and yet still the pressure for me to conform to a different way of leadership was immense. The resulting stress I felt increased the struggle and the striving, and life felt very, very hard and exhausting. The more I tried to resist the pressure to change, the more stress I felt because, at this time, I saw no solution.

CONVERSATIONS WITH MY SOUL

In our ways we understood the vital wisdom and experience that came from a lifetime; a lifetime of experiencing, a lifetime of discovering, a lifetime of learning, a lifetime of understanding, a lifetime of knowing. This came with walking upon the earth, it came with age, age was honoured, revered, respected, for there were many lessons that we could all discuss and learn from. This dissolved many, many centuries ago, for in the modern madness, it was seen that the young were the survival of the fittest, the energetic,

the productive and the profitable, that they were on
trend, up to date, visionary and beyond. And so, the
role of the woman leader almost became extinct and
if it survived it was time limited, as you know.

Unlike a graduate, fresh into the world of employment, the corporate structure could not control the mind from the outset. As it was, I did not see the sense in any of it, in the recruitment policies or processes. I felt like I was a square peg trying to fit into a round hole. The solution sought was to try to force a change in shape of the peg (person) when they should have focused on the hole (structure). A fluid, shape-shifting hole where pegs of all shapes and sizes could fit.

I saw from my own experiences, and from others around me, in many corporate environments that this constant trying to shove pegs into the wrong hole was detrimental to people's wellbeing. People being asked to step into roles not suited to their professional skills and most misaligned with their own passions, desires, needs and even persona, was causing dis-ease both physically and mentally. People kept stuck in roles they had outgrown or being pushed in any direction because it suited the bottom line. I personally experienced both scenarios. In the first scenario, I was kept stuck in a role for four years longer than I had agreed to be in it. I was excelling in it and so it suited the corporate agenda, which was based on profit over people, and suited the hierarchy immediately above me. This hierarchy sat at a level high enough to be in direct contact with the top of the structure that really did decide your future, and so were being noticed for the results I was delivering with my team further down the line (so those not in contact with the top of the structure).

In the second scenario, when I had reached a certain level of seniority within that structure, I was pushed in every which way, and was expected to be able take on any role or project given to me, even those I had no experience of, or expertise in. It made no sense to me, as if the job grade and the associated salary suddenly made me a master of everything. There was absolutely zero support. If you asked for help because you had zero experience in what was being asked of you, the corporate response was that this is expected of you at this level. It made no sense whatsoever and just created fear and stress. This was completely unjust.

I have seen so many cases where individuals are not given the opportunity to excel within their own potential because they are limited by the company or moulded into something they simply are not. Where people have been forced into roles or positions due to demands of the productivity and profit of the company. Where talented people leave roles and companies that they were so aligned to, where they were so connected to their colleagues and clients. You know the ones that leave a hole in the dynamics of the team when they go and its never quite the same without them. They are forced to leave roles that they excelled in and loved doing. Why? There is a disconnection with senior leaders, a structure that places people in boxes, above and below each other with little communication. Where the leaders do not know their people, a lack of care, the 'flow and let go' of people, and interference in the pursuit of more productivity/profit and a lack of human understanding and compassion.

As I see it, this backfires every time because, ultimately, the relationship breaks down. There is no honour and respect, the company pushes, demands and the person breaks. Often mental health issues arise, as their sense of self is diminished. Ultimately, no one wins, the company loses an asset, a talented individual who could have continued to excel for the company and become an inspiring leader for the next generation of employees. If you are or have experienced this, let me take a moment to reassure you that through the considerations of change I share in Chapter 11, this style of leadership can change.

CONVERSATIONS WITH MY SOUL

This approach may have sufficed but it will not in these changing times, people will want and expect more.

As a corporate employee you are the subject of a great deal of scrutiny and measurement against a predefined set of corporate measurements and benchmarks that come from the top down. These measurements are aligned with the corporate structure's agenda, which as I experienced is to deliver profit with little or no regard for the people who deliver that. The measurements are reviewed regularly, and you are then benchmarked against your own peers and ranked in order, from highest achiever to lowest achiever, and these results are made public for all to see.

Occasionally, you are also required to seek the feedback of senior leaders to see how you are measuring up in the eyes of others. The benchmark process I experienced, largely involved people who did not really even know me, score me against a set of predefined corporate concepts/definitions to ascertain if I was really any good or not. This, as I experienced, covered all aspects of the Self, even down to my appearance, which was to be more masculine ideally. I was told that I should wear my glasses more often because they 'made me look more serious'. I was subjected to this process in that I was assessed and scored. Also, as a leader myself, I was responsible for scoring others. I always felt a sense of detachment from the process. I think this was because I could see the pointlessness in that process, and to cope with the inhumanness of it as I see it now. As a leader, I would have to allocate these measurements and then present them upwards to the hierarchy above who did not even know the individual. A case for every score, which would then be scrutinised and either agreed or disagreed with; even though, as the person's manager, I was surely the one best placed to determine the accurate measure. These scores were used to ascertain how much, or if any, of the financial annual bonus reward pot you are entitled to.

I invite you to just pause and consider what concepts and definitions are set in your workplace for you to measure up against.

- Are they meaningful to you and to every individual within your company?
- Do they support and serve you and your teams?

- Do they promote productive, open, respectful two-way conversations without instilling fear or judgement?
- Do the systems and structures offer opportunity for equal progression for all or just those who measure up?
- How is team reward distributed?

The pressure placed on people was immense. It saddened me a great deal where I saw this pressure being applied to a young generation of graduates, eager to achieve their definition of success, no doubt a societal one like mine was. They were performance measured against a set of metrics, often unrelatable measurements, and then branded according to how they measured up against this set of criteria. They were either high performers, like a badge of honour, or under performers, like a brand of shame and each with its own specific clearly defined path to follow. To me it appeared regimented. These were young people with little experience of the world of work or wisdom gained from age and life experiences. As I saw it, there was no care, no gentle compassionate, guidance or considerate leadership offered as they transitioned from education to full time employment. Many of them I met were robotic and highly competitive. There was so much fear. I lost count of the number of female graduates who would reach out to me. They sought guidance, reassurance, kindness, a sense of connection, to share their fear and doubts openly and without judgement – fulfilment of their human needs.

CONVERSATIONS WITH MY SOUL

The human being has basic needs as you know; shelter, warmth, food, and then it has deeper needs. In order to truly be productive in potential and creation, they need to belong, to be treated with honour and respect and kindness and care. The human being needs to thrive through being given a sense of Self, a priority, an importance, a potential, a purpose, a presence. With respect and honour the human being becomes infinite in their production and their potential and will give back the same values. Yet there is little investment in the biggest resource, the person. If a person feels like nothing, they will behave like nothing.

This was an interesting channelling, as it highlights the deeper needs of a person, that I knew were not being met in my leadership experience, either by my Self or as I perceived by my team. In the end, I did sadly feel like nothing.

I look back now, and I see that the only real fulfilment my senior leadership role brought was this connection; this real human connection to these young people who sought advice from me, because they saw that I was different, in that despite my position, I was approachable. At the time I felt that it was wrong for me to be different, even though being approachable is clearly a good quality to have! I felt that my difference was a failing because I did not fit. I understand now that my sense of personal failure was less to do with my own personal shortcomings, which I did have an awareness of, and more to do with the system of power, control, and the culture I was surrounded by.

At the time, I could not understand the accolade and rewards presented to me for exceptional performance. In my mind, at the time, I was just applying common sense and that was all that was needed to create the change needed. I could see those relationships with the suppliers' providing services were broken or non-existent. There was no relating, there was no shared sense of goal, no commonality or working in unity. It was a case of 'them versus us', (aligned with the training I have shared with you) of appointing blame. There was fear within the team, so all sense of creativity was null and void. The pressure from the top to fix the situation was immense and the people at the bottom trying to fix it could not see, think, or feel differently because they had been programmed by the structure and systems of how to be. They were robotic, devoid of emotion, fearful to just be their Self, or to even relate openly to each other and to the suppliers. Even if they did see what needed to change, no one dared to 'stick their head above the parapet' and express. There was no time for them to pause, to stop and consider, to think, to get creative together to solve the problems. They were on the relentless corporate treadmill, where there is no concept of pausing for thought.

It was easy for me to create change and now that I am out of this environment, I see that this is because I had not been programmed at this early time of my career to think, feel, and behave as the corporate structure dictated. I was not controlled, and so I was not yet fearful, unlike my colleagues, and I related to people as my authentic Self. I was free to see where the root cause of the problem lay and to make the changes which all focused upon people, relating to people in an open, honest, and respectful way.

Several years later, at a time in that environment where I was consumed by the culture and full of fear, I was asked if I thought my style of management and leadership was better than this corporate way, as if it were some sort of competition. At the time I was shocked and wondered where this had come from. Although now I see it was probably due to my apparent and frustrating resistance to being controlled by the culture and to conform to a style of management that was wholly different to my own. However, as I was fearful of the consequences, of not toeing the corporate line that controlled, I had given a suitable self- derogatory, self-depreciating response to appease the more senior person. Now that I am out of this structure and no longer controlled by it or fearful of it, I consider that my response would now simply be, "Yes I do". This is not a judgemental response or me blowing my own trumpet so to speak, it is just a matter of fact.

To create change you have to stop feeding the misplaced and unconscious control. How? You may ask. I ask you to consider this:

What sits beneath control is fear,

what sits beneath fear is loss,

and what sits below loss is the SELF.

Through a process that I teach to leaders of self-identification, and self-actualisation, you consider for yourself the control you are in and the control that you are. For this is what creates the competition, the insecurity, the fear, the loss, the sheer insanity of relating in a way that holds the negative attributes of control, deception, manipulation, diminishment, denial, hierarchy. Then further through the process of consideration, conceptualisation, and emergence of the considerations for change that I share with you, the loss and the fear is eradicated so the need for control dissolves. As a leader, you are the one 'in control', the change starts with you, it all comes back to the Self.

Knowing your Self, eliminates the loss, which eliminates the fear, which eliminates the need for control, as a leader you are free to work in unity with everyone and it becomes clear that there is no need for competition, of who makes a better leader, there is no such concept. The 'I am it' and 'I am better than you', is eradicated. So, if you find yourself in a similar position, I would like to reassure you that this can change.

Let's talk for a moment about company values and ethics which are reflected in the company code of conduct.

CONVERSATIONS WITH MY SOUL

Many companies hold no trust and do not consider their values and whether they are implementing them or whether they are just for show.

In my experience within a corporate structure, training on these was militant, you would be tested on them regularly. Could you recite the company's code of conduct, values, ethics and did you know the consequences you faced if you were found to break them? In my view it was a meaningless HR tick box exercise to check off the to do list as there was no connection to these. Never was I asked to explain how these values related to me or whether they were indeed aligned to my own values. Particularly, given the leadership role I was responsible for, did I even understand them? It was like everything else I experienced; it was all fear-based. These are the company rules that are set, learn them, do not question them, abide by them, or face the consequences. A **discussion of these values** was not part of any interview process either, perhaps if they had been, both parties, certainly in my experience, would have realised that we did not fit with each other. We did not have the same concepts of the definition of leadership.

At the outset of my employment, and an important part of the considerations I had based my decision upon to move to one particular organisation, was the agreement I had made when recruited that I would carry out the role for a period of 4 years maximum. After that time, a move back to a marketing-based role would be supported, which was my real area of expertise and passion. This did not transpire. Why not? I felt it was because it suited the business needs to keep me in the role I was in, stuck because the need for profit came before my needs.

I felt really let down and undervalued. It was apparent that what I wanted or needed for my own sense of personal fulfilment, growth, and happiness were not of any relevance. There was a mindset from the leadership above me that it was job rank and earnings that were the key to fulfilment, growth, and happiness, and as I was climbing the ranks and increasing my salary, how could there be an issue?

I was often asked if I knew how successful I was, reminded of how much money I was earning in the form of bonuses or performance related shares. This was the corporate, societal definition of success, not mine. I felt sad as I realised the words agreed at the outset of my employment and which had really been a deal breaker for me, were meaningless. It made me question the ethics and values of trust and integrity. I realised that although I had never really defined my own values, and although the company values of honesty, integrity and respect sounded good written on paper, they were not understood or applied because the hierarchical structure was misaligned to these values. More importantly no one took any responsibility for them. They were written and published for all to see but I wondered who had written them and when. When I checked they were created over 40 years ago! I hear you say, somewhat outdated then.

In these sorts of structures and systems, there is no two-way conversation. As the employee you are not asked to consider these concepts of company ethos, ethics, values for yourself and yet these form the building blocks of the structure and systems that you are expected to become and lead within. You are not asked if you understand them, or if you agree with them, and so I did not consider them and, more often than not, I could not even relate to them, as I feel is the case for many. Sadly, as this continued to play out in my own experiences it transpired that the code of conduct was not worth the paper it was written on.

These values and integrating them into every part of your business is vital for long term sustainability. By this I mean the identification of how people are treated, respected, honoured - is it in line with the company ethics, ethos, code of conduct, and values?

CHAPTER 7

Reputation and Recommendation

To ATTRACT THE RIGHT people, I believe that leaders need to know their own values, values that are directly linked to the Self, values of kindness, care, and compassion for the people that they lead. These form the values of the company for which they represent. It is these values that form your own and the company's reputation.

CONVERSATIONS WITH MY SOUL

It is the leader's responsibility, the leader is 'able to respond'. A response to the 'why' of all the people with integrity, discernment, personal and professional and people centred responsibility to all things.

101

This is an emotional and mindful commencement of a deeper connection to product and purpose that will automatically begin to ignite a sense of fulfilment.

Reputation

For many, the word 'corporate' conjures up negative words or emotions; corporate agenda, corporate identity, corporate culture, corporate hierarchy, corporate persona, corporate training, corporate treadmill, to toe the corporate line, and corporate slavery. For those who are in it, more often than not, they want to get out of it but feel trapped or at dis-ease with themselves, like I did. This is because of the corporate identity that consumes you and the money and the material that is used in exchange for your Self - your true identity. Like my colleague said to me, you may likely feel like you are 'selling your soul'.

Many larger corporates do not have a good reputation, often the company ethics and conduct are considered questionable. It does not surprise me that many young people are seeking alternative definitions of success and creating their own businesses. There is a greater awareness of the trade off in work/life balance that is made when you choose this path. It will likely bring success if your definition of success is based on the material. If it is based upon the societal definition of success, and this is an individual choice but with today's corporate concepts of leadership it often comes at a cost. This is unacceptable, leading the next generation as they start their working lives should be seen as a great responsibility. There should be care and compassion to help each individual to discover and reach the pinnacle of their potential, not to suppress their potential by enforcing concepts that confine them, to thrive not to just survive. As a leader it is your responsibility to be awake and to know that you are responsible for all of these people. I invite you to pause and consider for a moment and ask yourself, how do the existing concepts of leadership serve you?

I am asking you to consider your being, because as a leader this is the only way you can open up and be awake to consider the being of another.

CONVERSATIONS WITH MY SOUL

A reputation is what comes from your responsibility and your structure. If you look at what the facets of responsibility are; responsibility to people, potential, the opening to opportunities, the provision, the protection, being reputable, a reputation, a representa-

tion of a person, and what that person represents, their reputation has little understanding.

In today's world there is little understanding of the word reputation. A company or a person has a reputation for their product or service, and this is represented by a brand or strapline. But this is not the true meaning of the word reputation. Reputation is not about being known for the offering or a brand or strapline, this is merely a lip service. Reputation is earned by the person and represented through structures that serve and take responsibility of all people.

A representation is a presentation of a person's why, depth, character, and spirit. Look at external circumstances and what people are demanding and wanting and the change that is coming from external circumstances in a time of a pandemic, people expect and want more. For a company to excel, it is their reputation of the whole and who is responsible for the whole? The leader is responsible.

And, therefore, what those leaders represent and do and implement through their company, is not in their words or language but in the sanctioning of their action, their values, their opportunities, training, development, ethos, ethics, structure, accountability, responsibility, and communication.

Knowing it is a reputation, a representation of that company and what they represent to their employee, to their customers, to the whole and beyond is vital.

A reputation has a responsibility socially and culturally to care, to give back, to be involved, not to just have the words.

The rising of the fittest is not those that earn more, do more, achieve more, expand more, trample on, the survival from solidarity to sustainable success comes from the reputation, the representation of that company. And only can the representation be sought through going into the depths of discovery, of deep emotional, mindful, physical, spiritual even - meaning of their why.

For as it was in my experiences, there is no reputation because there is nothing to represent. Exploitation, diminishment, greed, how can one represent that? Companies will need to consider change because a conscious reputation becomes even more important in these different times.

CONVERSATIONS WITH MY SOUL

A reputation, a representation of both company and leaders, can only truly come through a change in structure and a change in responsibility.

An ability to respond to the structure and to the company and to considerations for change and a new concept being formed. Only then can a more people

*centred approach that will excel the reputation organ-
ically begin to form.*

*For a reputation is earned, a true, sustainable reputa-
tion is earned not given. Reputations are given lightly
through labels and titles. In these times of rising consciousness, people cannot be deceived or fooled as
they will know when a representation of the company
or the individual has been earned. A true reputation
that is earned through concepts and considerations
for change, it is the only way to earn it, you earn
something through doing it.*

*As economic uncertainty prevails, the survival is on
those companies who connect and collaborate and are
secure enough to take joint venture partnership initiatives. For companies to excel, a reputation that naturally gives trust, responsibility, accountability,
opportunity, and structure, is what is needed for other
collaborators and companies to consider a partnership. If a company is in competition, out for themselves, they cannot relate, cannot honour their values,
cannot respect another, there will be a reluctance to
collaborate. Solidarity is what creates sustainable
success, not singular. It must be done on all levels,
from small companies to large.*

We are already seeing there are collaborations happening where one company is selling
another and vice versa. We are already seeing

companies intermingle with their service, stock, and production to excel a collective profit.

CONVERSATIONS WITH MY SOUL

These kind of collaborates will be seen and will grow on a more intense level bringing opportunities to many. If the representation from the senior leadership and the reputation of the company is not there, a consideration for a collaboration will be dismissed in these uncertain times.

External forces are creating change and so there is little company choice as we see the changes in economic results and climate. The climate will create a consciousness that will connect and so the survival of the perceived fittest is not those that compete and trample upon, but those that connect through these considerations for change, and that allow a deeper meaning of the why to be presented.

Reputation is a key to certainty, certainty is a key to the creation of a secure, conscious company.

Recommendation

CONVERSATIONS WITH MY SOUL

Without a reputation there is no recommendation. Recommendation is to commend - re - repeat, repeat, recommend, commendation, and about people relating. People cannot reach out, give, share, when there is a limited sense of self and self-esteem.

In these structures that I have experienced, there is a fear-based energy where once again it is about 'me' and 'out for me'. There is little understanding of the power of the people and the power of the word that will repeat a commendation again and again and again.

CONVERSATIONS WITH MY SOUL

Regardless of investment, regardless of PR it is people! It is their support, it is their service, it is their custom and yet there is little put into the making of relationships that will repeat a commendation again, again and again. No consideration, no responsibility, little action or plan into the power and recommendation and repeat custom through giving, sharing, community and collaboration.

Commend, it is indeed an honour to be commended, a recommendation is to recommend over, and over again. Because one or plural have earned the right to their commendation and is recommended for the consistent commitment to the considerations for change that bring all people together.

Where everyone wins, no one misses out and everyone survives and everyone gains a bit of someone else's success, because those that have it share their extra bit with someone else. Creating more solidarity, more sustainability, more success based on connection, consideration, it is devoid of competition and the notion that those that have more, have won, this is not the case. To keep recommending is to keep responding in responsibility to a new way of leadership, new concepts that allows the reputation to form into a commendation that is always re-established. This way of being yields an organic production for a recommendation, it is spontaneous, it is word of mouth, it is connection, it is referral, and it is a desire to want to connect, to relate.

A recommendation is relating, it is a relationship - recommending someone, company to company. It is a connection and therefore is not pushed, strived for, or having to achieve. It is given to somebody, commended. It is a gift, and it is earned. When a company is commended, the connections appear and will appear and allows them more success.

This is a simple formula that I share with you and it all stems from the considerations for change that I go into more detail in the next part of this book. The change in structure, responsibility and reputation leads to what I am writing about. Recommendation, being commended for the work done, allows many to want to relate. When you relate in this way you create, when you create you are productive, when you are productive you are profitable. It is only through this way for sustainable success to be brought forth.

CONVERSATIONS WITH MY SOUL

The world of work and business will have to relate more with others in a more shared way where everyone gains, and everyone receives. It is the only way to survive external circumstances. It is a way that has a capability and a capacity to bring more. The trampling on another is outmoded and will become yesterday's consciousness very quickly. Companies will want to be known for what they can offer, their initiatives, their incentives and staff sustainability, rewards, promotions, profit share.

I invite you to please take a moment to pause and to consider what is being communicated here. For I appreciate that I have shared a great deal of channelled wisdom in the pages of this chapter.

To put it more plainly, at some point the unacceptable has become acceptable in the concepts that create the systems and structures that the majority of people work within. I do not dispute that there are some companies that are far more conscious in their leadership, but for most there is no conscious leadership because there is no awareness of the need for change. Sadly, on a wider level within the systems and structure that lead and govern our world this is apparent. You do not need my words for you can see the unacceptable being accepted all around you.

Leadership needs to change, and that change simply starts with your consideration of the Five Facets of the Self.

CHAPTER 8

Diminishment

AS I BECAME MORE senior in position and delivered more and more, 'to deliver with a laser light focus', being the corporate motto, rather than feeling more supported I felt more and more suppressed and fearful. I was aware of this intense pressure for me to conform and change but why and for what? I initially wasn't sure. I could not understand why I needed to change, to present myself differently, particularly because I was highly regarded for my leadership and results. As I have shared, the results I had delivered for the company had largely been through my ability to relate to others openly and authentically without a sense of hierarchy, the 'I am it', and to lead within my own concepts.

There was immense pressure for me to think, feel and behave in a way that was alien to me and to display behaviours that are completely opposed to my own set of values and sense of fairness. I noticed this pressure really came into force and that it all started to unravel for me personally, within this structure, when I was recognised as a high performer following my promotion, the one where I had been told that I had sold my soul. I was showing all the promising traits of a leader who could go all the way, right to the very top of the company.

Through the culture of continually being measured and benchmarked against my peers, a results driven culture where one's goals are all aligned with the structures agenda of more profit, I had reached the point where I stood out as being worthy of this high accolade. Described to me as an honour, which involved the recognition from a very important HR person and a significant financial investment. I was told that I had been 'selected' for attending a leadership programme reserved only for the elite few, who displayed all the right qualities necessary for reaching the very top of the company. It was at this point that the unconsciousness within me really started to become more conscious.

What do I mean by this? I started to have an awareness of a concept of leadership that did not serve, support, or fit me, and that possibly this was the cause of the pain and the dis-ease that I was starting to feel. I started to see and feel the real agenda, the final stages of my conversion. I felt like I was being programmed to be a senior leader where all aspects of that concept of leadership were against the very core of my being. At this point, I began to feel my own diminishment, my fear deepened, and I felt a sense of impending doom. I really struggled with this at the time because, although I had a sense of awareness, this feeling was quite the opposite of what I expected to be feeling having reached this point of my career, of what I had been conditioned to think about how I should be feeling.

Despite this deep sense that I had of the injustice and the unfairness, and because I was coming from a place of fear, a need to survive and so like everyone I perceived around me I must strive to survive, I continued to 'toe the corporate line' in a very subservient and almost unconscious way. I believed, at that time, that I was not enough, I was full of imposter syndrome and thought that in order to be successful I must change. I was too fearful to challenge, to stand up and be different, too fearful of the concepts and systems that constrained me and to just be my Self.

Having felt controlled and conditioned by the culture, I reluctantly, and feeling sick with anxiety at the very prospect of becoming this sort of leader, started the programme. As I had come to expect, there was no real connection with any of the other attendees because it just felt so inhuman, devoid of emotion, no support and it was highly competitive. There was no sense of solidarity or connection with each other. No shared excitement or sense of united responsibility for becoming inspiring leaders for future generations, just a focus on the financial reward, the title, the status, to be the best person on the programme, and to meet or exceed the expectations placed on you by the hierarchy above. Many of these colleagues had been recruited straight from graduation and as such had gone through years of the corporate conditioning required to meet the grade, so perhaps they felt differently to me, but my senses told me otherwise.

With awareness, I see now that I did not want to be moulded into a predefined concept of a leader, into someone else's concept, in an outdated hierarchical structure where I felt values were meaningless and that I now felt completely suppressed by. I found myself several months later coming into an awareness of the fact that I had indeed sold my soul. I started at this point to reconsider my definition of success as I realised that I did not want to become this leader that I was on the corporate treadmill to become. I had been stripped bare of any sense of Self, devoid of emotion, leading with little compassion, care, or consideration of others because it had become too painful to feel.

The dis-ease that I was feeling really started to manifest. It started to show up as a debilitating sense of fear. The ego told me it was my fault and I felt like this because I was not good enough to lead at this level. I consciously would avoid speaking my mind or asking questions. I felt huge discomfort during board meetings when we each in turn would be asked to speak and present to those more senior, to ourselves. I had no self-confidence and became literally terrified at the prospect of any public speaking where I had to stand up and stand out in front of the disconnected hierarchy above, it was like my kryptonite. I was so terrified of failing to meet the demands of this culture. At this point, I had no sense of my own identity, and I was failing miserably at becoming the corporate leader identity that was expected. As I have already shared, I started to take betablockers prescribed by a doctor to calm my anxiety, the self-medicating behaviours to numb down what I was really feeling, the crying out of my spirit.

I was so fearful because I knew I was being constantly compared to others, to these senior leaders that I could not relate to on any level. People who did not know me, that I had been conditioned by the structure and leadership to fear. I also had seen the unfairness and the injustice and so I knew that my success depended constantly upon how I measured up to the powers that be, the hierarchy of leaders that sat above me. I became ashamed of who I was and attempted to encase my own identity in a fake veneer that others would find impressive and pleasing. I watched a couple of close colleagues move faster up the ranks than I did because they conformed. I watched them change from themselves into these serious, robotic characters that no longer had the time of day for any personal interaction. At first, it bemused me and then as it was continually pointed out to me that I needed to be like them, I felt very fearful. I was told that these characteristics were expected of me at this job level. I was repeatedly told that I needed to fit in by changing, that I needed to be seen, and to be visible by senior management now I was at this level. I did not understand these comments about needing to be seen because it was surely through being seen that I had been able to climb the corporate ladder and be promoted to this level. I had met the criteria required for this ongoing upwards climb of the career ladder by displaying my own characteristics, so why now, upon this promotion, did I need to change into this robotic version of myself?

I really did not understand and so I really tried hard to please. I started to adopt the robotic corporate persona, the need to appear strictly professional and serious at all times. A professional persona that makes one appear impersonable, unrelatable, the joyless persona I mentioned in the previous chapter. I became this way for some time, unrelatable to others as much as I was to myself at that time. I tried to be devoid of any emotion or show any emotional intelligence in my leadership and in doing so, I lost more of my Self. So strong was the corporate persona in this culture that I was once asked by a supplier who saw me as different, if my colleagues were like sticks of rock? If one were ever to break them in half were they corporate branded through to their very core?

I wondered what was wrong with me. Why couldn't I change? Why did I fear the leadership programme so much? Why was I so fearful? I had no role models to turn to, and of the very few women in more senior positions that I was exposed to, I felt a desperate sense of fear of becoming one of them, rather than any aspiration to become like them. It felt like there was no feminine presence within the structure or systems and by that, I mean no compassion, no kindness, no care, no friendly advice. I had no support.

CONVERSATIONS WITH MY SOUL

Let me speak of what I see, of what you have experienced, is there really a feminine in the workplace, in the corporate, in the company, is there really? These women have been conditioned to become the same as the structure. To think, feel and behave as the concepts required, in order to survive, this is the only way.

You either succumb to the masculine concepts and control, which means letting go of your Self, or you walk away. There is no other way to be, for the systems and the structure do not support the feminine leader. In a male dominated world women have lost their greatest connection, supporting each other.

I had been made to fear senior leaders and so it wasn't an option to knock on the door of a friendly manager or HR colleague for the guidance, care, compassion, sense of connection and solidarity I was desperately seeking. I felt so alone. At this level of seniority, I was constantly reminded that this struggle I was having was most definitely regarded as being a huge personal failing, a weakness, a completely unacceptable way of being and I had better pull myself together or else.

As I carried around the heavy weight of this fake veneer I had encased myself within, I started to experience panic attacks and then a sense that I was shutting down, emotionally and physically, slowly, bit by bit, like my senses were fading and becoming blurred. I couldn't think straight. I felt like I could barely function and then overwhelmed by a sense of pointlessness, I stopped caring, devoid of any emotion for others within that environment.

"The reward for conformity is that everyone likes you but yourself"

Rita Mae Brown

I was robotic in my duties and filled with an overwhelming sense of self-loathing. I recall a colleague who had worked for me for over ten years telling me during a social drink after work that she didn't think she would like me very much if she had only met me now. Powerful words to hear at the time and I replied to say that I pretty much agreed with her. I didn't much like myself either. This is what happens when you become so disconnected to your authentic Self, when you, day in and day out, play a role that is so far removed from who you actually are. If you resonate with this, please consider the Five Facets of the Self, consider the concepts for change. Know that just in this process you create awareness, and as I have shared awareness is transformative, and so you can create change that will enable you to identify and to be your authentic Self. It is important before we consider anything that we firstly consider ourselves. If you do not even like your Self this is a sure sign that you deserve to give to your Self the time out, the stop, to consider your Self.

It may come as no surprise for me to share with you that I was experiencing in addition to my serious fertility issues, other physical illnesses at this time. I could not sleep and was constantly ill with IBS symptoms and oddly I would dry heave and feel like I was going to be physically sick most mornings before heading into the office. It was stress related anxiety and would happen when I felt particularly fearful. I felt imprisoned and trapped and saw no escape route at all. I had woken up to the fact of how unhappy at work I was, and how unauthentic I was in my leadership. At this time, I did not know how to find my Self, I did not have any considerations for change to consider. As I have mentioned, on the corporate treadmill you cannot consider anything other than to breathe, to keep your head above the water and survive. I felt completely exhausted during this period of my life. So miserable was I with the person I had become, this false identity I was playing out day in and day out.

This is a very personal extract from words channelled to me, I am sharing because they are the truth and I know for many it is a reality and it doesn't have to be.

CONVERSATIONS WITH MY SOUL

As you look back, you can acknowledge the pain, but when you were living that it was as if you were drowning in it, fighting to come up for air, to breathe for survival. As you looked at what was happening all around you, you thought what is the point? What is the point in all of this? What's the point of being here? What's the point of the pain? What's the point in trying to create change? What's the point? You are agreeing with my words, for I am speaking to your spirit. And therefore, it diminished your purpose because your purpose become erased, where the only purpose was to get out because then you were out of the pain, the drowning, the trying to swim to keep your head above water, to breathe. This is the illness, for you have to succumb to that way which does mean letting go of your Self and drowning into a sea of misplaced systems and structures. You didn't pay the price, you weren't prepared to pay the price, to sell your Soul, to diminish your sense of Self. You walked away. So, you didn't collude, and they didn't control, and you were free to let the scars heal and the wounds mend.

I was conforming to the concepts. I had blindly just toed the corporate line, not to think, feel or behave differently, nor to question the concepts that confined me, constricted me, conditioned me, and that frightened me into the submission of control. A masculine control in this experience. Although I had clearly reached the point where I was now experiencing the physical effects of my diminishment of the Self, I was still submissive to the controls, so saturated to the skin was I of the concepts of a corporate structure, that I did nothing. I was silenced and frozen by the fear.

Divine intervention was once more responsible for my alternative path. Due to an issue with my eventual successful pregnancy, I was unable to travel and as such I was not able to fully participate in the leadership programme. I may have been unconscious at the time of the real reasons for my fear, but my spirit knew. I did not want to become any more senior in that corporate environment.

Despite my very valid medical reasons for withdrawing from the programme, I unleashed a storm that I knew was coming. I was also now about to become a mother, so I had placed myself further outside of the corporate concepts of senior leadership. A wave of intense bullying was brought down upon me like a tsunami.

Such was the force that I was completely paralysed with fear and my transition back to work after maternity leave was made impossible for me. I was made to feel utterly pointless as my corporate identity and role, which due to my own unconsciousness and fear was all I really identified with of myself at that time, was literally stripped from me. I endured discriminatory comments as assumptions were made and vocalised that my recent motherhood limited me in my capacity to perform my role. The system saw to it that because I did not fit the concepts, because there was resistance from me to succumb to the cultural control and concepts of leadership, I was to be manoeuvred out. And so it began, it was made an impossible task for me to transition back into the workplace. I was passed from pillar to post, mislead, ignored, shouted at, bullied, disrespected, and offered no support. To all intents and purposes I accepted the unacceptable.

My team and my suppliers were left in utter confusion as to why I was not being placed back in my role. I had no answers, nor could I get any. It was humiliating. I was disregarded, disrespected, disempowered, diminished, denied, and dissociated with, even by close colleagues, friends even. They were too fearful to remain in contact with the outlawed person I had become. These are strong words, but this is my experience, and I felt the full force of punishment for refusing to sell my soul and for my rite of passage into motherhood. For being different in my leadership and for, unconsciously at the time, trying to free myself from the constraints of a structure that shackled me.

CONVERSATIONS WITH MY SOUL

So, place your strength, your spirit, your intuition, to strengthen another and to give to her the gift of having a fluid expression, unconditional, raw, authentic, honest, truthful, respectful. Free from the constraints of structure that shackles basic human rights. Silenced through the system, and silent in your sense of Self. Silent for the fear of their power resonates through every cell, every bone, your blood, every muscle, stuck and shackled disempowered, diminished, denied, disassociated with. A demise of human rights, the death is the penalty and the punishment.

I would literally dread waking up each morning, panic rising in me which grew stronger every day, from the fearful thoughts rushing round my head. Would they get rid of me? Why was this happening to me? Would we survive without my salary? I was the breadwinner at that time. Fear rising in me as I worried about not being able to pay our mortgage, losing our home and on a deeper level still, who would I be? My job defined me, didn't it? It was all I knew how to be. I kept asking myself how I could truly identify with another version of myself. This corporate experience had stripped me bare of any sense of my Self. I had no identity other than the role, the title, the job. I felt I would be nothing. I quite literally felt terrified and alone and daren't voice my fears. I was fearful of being judged or seen as being ungrateful, after all wasn't I one of those career women who 'had it all'? My inner child was very triggered at this time as I sought some form of support, solidarity outside of my Self, looking for others to help ease my pain and to tell me I wasn't alone. Although none was forthcoming at that time, not in that environment, no one dared offer me any support.

I know now that I am not alone in these thoughts I experienced at this time. The thoughts of 'I'm alone' – 'I'm alone in my worthlessness, in my pain', is part of a collective pain of women and this needs to change. Some two months into returning to work, I would find myself working alone from home sobbing at my desk, enormous waves of grief, panic and fear shuddering out of me so desperate was I to change my path but feeling trapped and seeing no escape route.

I looked around at all that was happening around me and I thought 'what's the point? What is the point in all of this? What's the point of being here? What's the point of the pain? What's the point in any of it?' I felt that my wings had been clipped, and even, on one occasion, used this term to describe how I felt, for which I was made to feel utterly ashamed for this display of emotion. I clearly saw that the structure lacked fairness and opportunities and support. I understood that I wasn't viewed as a person. I was nothing more than a piece of paper with a number on it that could be replaced by more paper.

I had reached a point when in despair I was literally shouting out loud to the Universe, to please get me off this path I had chosen, to please HELP ME.

During this time, my Mum told me about a lady who gave soul readings. So desperate was I for any kind of guidance, I once again set off on a more alternative approach of self-help. I got in touch with a lady called Sascha via telephone and then I waited to receive her reading, hoping it would provide some clarity, and some answers. As I sat and listened to the recording of my personal soul reading, I felt this deeper understanding of my Self. She explained that my soul is very peaceful and resonates with compassion for others, joy, and peace. All very female characteristics but from childhood I had struggled with the transition into womanhood (this is hugely accurate and is at least another chapter I could write about).

I had not learned to set any personal boundaries so had left myself wide open to takers and abusers. Being bullied was a repeat pattern from the age of eleven right up to that current time. I had no voice and as such could not say 'No'. So deep was my need for peace that often, I would allow bad things to happen to me because I would fear upsetting the other person by saying 'No'. I had zero feelings of self-worth. She told me that I had been playing to my masculine energy for so long that it had over-taken and I was so out of touch with my female attributes that I truly resonate with, particularly in my leadership. I had given away all my power and as a result I was out of balance, which was manifesting itself in all aspects of my life. She told me that life did not have to be this hard and that I could and would change this.

Out of the entire reading this gave me the most comfort, at the time. I cried with hope that my life wouldn't always feel so hard and so painful. She explained that I was not allowing my authenticity to shine and through traumatic experiences of loss and having my true sense of self stripped from me within my workplace, I had disconnected from my soul. I needed to re-connect. Over the following weeks, still feeling sceptical, it was all rather woo-woo for me to truly consider at the time, but desperate to try anything to feel better, I worked with her on a series of affirmations aimed at reconnecting me to my soul and understanding who I truly was. I found that the overwhelming sense of fear I was literally choking on at the time eased a little. However, I still did not have sight of an alternative path.

CHAPTER 9

The Stop

*"Once you make a decision, the Universe conspires
to make it happen"*

Ralph Waldo Emerson

THEN IT HAPPENED. THE Universe delivered the STOP I had literally been pleading for. Have you ever had one of those moments? A fork in the road, an alternative path was presented. It most certainly wasn't an easy one, but I realise now that it was the opportunity for me to finally wake up, to become conscious and to find my true Self. To step out of the pain and dis-ease that had become my normality.

My son was fifteen months old, and I had been back at work for just a few months. As I have shared, I had started to feel sick in the morning upon waking and so I had initially put this down to the sheer anxiety I felt going to work each day. Then I had this sinking realisation that I had experienced these symptoms before, when pregnant with my son. I could not possibly be pregnant. I had had a fallopian tube removed, the other was damaged having already suffered an ectopic pregnancy within it and the subsequent surgery. I was also a few months shy of my 40th birthday and I had been told that my chances of conceiving naturally were pretty much zero. It just wasn't going to happen. It was a miracle that IVF had finally worked.

I had however defied medical odds again and was informed I was six weeks pregnant and this time, a very early scan, confirmed that the pregnancy was in the correct place. I could hardly believe this news and felt such elation. Given my history, I was sent for another scan at the local NHS hospital where I had given birth not many months before. I went on my own, telling a colleague at work I had a short appointment and that I would be back in time to chair a conference call later that day at 2pm. As soon as I saw the sonographer's face, I let out a wail of anguish, they had been mistaken, the pregnancy sac was indeed in the last remaining fallopian tube. I was rushed to theatre within two hours of arriving, with what would sadly be the last of my many unsuccessful pregnancies, a third and final ectopic pregnancy.

I had this overriding sense that I needed to have the surgery performed in Sheffield and by my IVF consultant and previous surgeon, Mr Li. I asked my husband to call him, and he confirmed he could fit me in for surgery immediately and asked me to get over to Sheffield as soon as possible. However, as my husband was sharing this with me, the senior nurse asked to speak to my consultant and took my husband's phone. Once she had hung up, she knelt in front of the chair I was slumped in and put her kind face very close to mine. She told me that the test results she had just seen suggested that I may not survive the short journey from Chesterfield Royal to the Sheffield Thornbury Hospital, even if I travelled by ambulance, such was the severity. I already had signs of internal bleeding and surgery was urgent. I was going to have to get to theatre now. In order to calm me, she took my hand in hers and reassured me that she would ensure I was moved into one of her comfortable private rooms within the maternity ward and she would look after me during recovery. I was put onto a theatre trolley and pushed along to theatre feeling complete and utter shock and very alone.

I woke up and I was in a bed, wearing my glasses. Everything looked white and very bright, and my grandma was sat at the bottom of my bed reaching her hand out to me. She looked the same as she did the last time I saw her, before she passed away, smiling at me with love and warmth, so pleased to see me and with her bad leg stretched out in front of her on a footstool. I remember trying to sit up and reach her hand and felt as though I was moving towards her but then, as I looked harder and kept trying to reach her, she seemed to be moving further away. The distance between us was not changing, despite me feeling myself moving towards her. Suddenly after what felt like quite some time had passed, she was sitting in the bay opposite me. "Grandma?" I heard myself say but maybe this was in my imagination. I realised it wasn't my grandma, but an elderly lady I didn't recognise. Suddenly my senses all rushed back to me. I sat up and felt immense pain, and there were elderly people all around me, one was groaning loudly. I needed to get up, what was I doing here? Panic rising, I saw a nurse and asked her to help me to get up as I needed to get ready for work and get on with my normal morning routine.

She allowed me to get out of bed, which I re-alised, and she soon did, that she shouldn't have. It was at the moment that I realised, much to my horror, that I was attached to a machine on wheels, that I part dragged across the floor before I almost collapsed to the ground. She caught me and helped me to lie back down, as more nurses were suddenly appearing from all directions to assist. I realised I had tubes all over me, and there were bloodstains on the bed sheets that I was lying on. I started to sob, where was I? Why was I in so much pain? Where was my little boy? Where was my husband? I was given some medication and I fell asleep. When I awoke, the senior nurse from the previous day came to see me. She apologised profusely for the fact that I was on a ward, and she informed me that my laparoscopy keyhole surgery to remove my pregnancy and remaining fallopian tube had gone terribly wrong. I still, to this day, do not know the exact details. I think at the time I found it too traumatic to comprehend and now it doesn't matter.

During a laparoscopy, to gain access to the body parts they need to operate upon, a fine needle is inserted through an incision next to your belly button. Then gas is pumped into the space to separate your abdominal wall from your organs so that camera and necessary instruments can be inserted. It was during this stage that they suspected they had perforated my bowel. My vital statistics being monitored at the time certainly seemed to suggest this was the case. Therefore, another specialist surgeon was drafted in immediately who proceeded to perform the open surgery necessary in order ascertain if perforation had occurred. Thankfully, it had not. If it had, I would not be here writing this today. The nurse explained that I had had extremely invasive surgery and, as a result, been put on a ward so I could be monitored closely during the night. I don't know how much of this I had taken in at that point.

I recall being in a state of utter shock, disbelief and a kind of numbness had taken hold. I was also in a great deal of post-surgery pain; unlike anything I had ever experienced before. She left me then, with promises to get me moved to a more comfortable environment later that day, as I could expect to be in hospital for several days.

I was unable to move or do a great deal for myself for at least the six weeks that followed. I couldn't even hold my child. I withdrew from everything and everyone as I felt so full of guilt for all the hurt that I had caused everyone around me, and it affected me very badly that I was missing out on caring for my son. I felt all the life, literally drain out of me. It was at this time that my GP diagnosed me with depression, wrote me a prescription and signed me off work for a short period of time. I instinctively knew that no medication would heal me, the journey I needed was much deeper than that. I needed to heal my soul.

As I lay in my bed gripped by this dark feeling of complete emptiness, I suddenly became aware of this overwhelming sense of wellbeing and love that I had connected with many times, but only ever momentarily, during my IVF journey, that I shared with you in Chapter 3. Here it was manifesting inside me, despite the utter darkness I felt consumed by. The tears of pain flowing uncontrollably down my face, suddenly turning to tears of blissful joy and this heavy debilitating feeling in my body turning to lightness, so light that I felt I could almost float away.

As I observed these feelings, these emotions which overtook my body, I realised that my mind and brain were not controlling these intense blissful feelings. I knew that this inner peace must be coming from my soul. I then felt a hand, an invisible hand that lifted mine from the bedcovers and held it tight. I was overcome by the deepest sense of being loved and safe that it took my breath away. I remember trying to lie so still and not move so as not to frighten it away. I felt so at peace in those moments and, as strange as it may sound, I recognised it was my grandma's hand who had passed away a year earlier.

It was really this experience that eradicated any remaining sense of scepticism, and when I stopped trying to apply logic to the number of rather spiritual experiences I had accumulated throughout this period of my life. I lay there holding this hand that I could not see but could very clearly feel with every other sense of my being and knew that everything I needed to change was within me. It was as if a lightbulb had lit up in my mind. I would take the courageous and brave steps necessary to make the massive life changes I needed to make. This sense of clarity overriding the fear that had quite literally floored me and, in that moment, I knew what I needed to do. I had a strength inside me and although I knew that the path ahead would be difficult, I also knew in that moment I was fully supported, and the Universe had my back. Whatever would happen, I would be OK.

PART 2

CONSCIOUS

CHAPTER 10

Identification

In this pause began the process of my own identification. I realised that I had never paused for thought, for consideration or identification of myself. In our lost ways of work, a fast-track world, long hours, and little health there is little food for thought. There is little intelligence for how the being in the human truly desires to be.

CONVERSATIONS WITH MY SOUL

Wholeness comes through a change in conscious, consciousness means awareness. Consciousness can only change, and awakening can only take place when you are prepared to explore.

In our world of analysing, psychology, psychotherapy, and whilst I am not disputing the power of these philosophies, there is success in simplicity. Through setting time and space for your Self, through creating a pause, when you ask the being in the human; the human knows the answer. The intellect is inside and often does not need the therapy. The being within needs a space for connection, collaboration, creation where the being, the inner being can truly express its needs, its wants, and its desires.

As I have recalled my experiences and look back to my Self at that time I knew, I intuitively knew, innately knew, what my being needed. It was speaking, screaming even, but I was not listening to it. It was only in the pause when I stopped, that I heard it and allowed it to be heard. I also had an awareness that it was not the therapy or the anti-depressants that I needed, it was the pause, the stop to consider my Self. Have you had that feeling in your life? Did you listen?

I saw that I had spent a lifetime of going through the motions being led by beliefs and conditioning that did not serve me. I was working with concepts of leadership that were at complete opposites with my own concepts, my own values, and my own ethics, of how I relate to others, just without awareness of this at the time. The problem was not solely with me or my leadership. I was not an imposter, it was the outdated corporate structures and systems that diminish people, that place profit at any cost afore all else, that was where the crux of the problem lay.

When I did stop, I saw that the answers were inside me and I had a choice. I could choose to stop accepting what was unacceptable to me, because it had become so unacceptable it had become unbearable. I knew from what I had experienced that there was a part of me that was strong and that I had gone through so much and was still fighting for survival. I considered what did I want to survive for? What was I struggling and striving for? I did not know my purpose at that time, but I did know that it wasn't this painful existence that was for sure. I felt a sense of love and respect for myself, for this part of my Self, the Spirit of me, that for most of my life I had been unaware of. I had an idea that if I started to work on connecting more with this part of my Self I would start to heal and feel a lot better.

I began to consider my Self, just a little as I was so fearful and suffering from poor mental health, but it was a start. This is what I am asking you to do. I do hope that what I have learned through my experiences and the channelled wisdom that has been spoken to me will help you to consider your own Self. That you will consider this new mode of leadership, so a conscious way of leadership can become the way forward.

I considered if I could survive without the role and the title, because the role to all intents and purposes had been taken from me already. Could I survive without the money, the material, my home. There was a clear voice that came from within me that responded "Yes", of course I could. They could take it all, the title, the role, the position, the money but they would not take my Spirit. It simply was not theirs to take.

As I contemplated the enormity of these thoughts, I felt the waves of panic at the realisation of how these thoughts needed to manifest and the action I needed to take. However, in between these waves, was a more intense and deeper fear that was being brought into my awareness. That of remaining stuck within the confines of this structure and this culture, which overrode the fear of stepping into the unknown with no clear path ahead.

"And then the day came when the risk to stay in bud was more painful than the risk it took to blossom"

Anais Nin

With much courage, I stood up and I stood out and I spoke my truth. I raised a formal grievance and presented my case for review, hoping that it would be considered and that the concepts of leadership that I had experienced would be reviewed. I hoped that the unfairness and the injustice would be considered and addressed within the structures and the systems. I hoped that there would be change in the outdated corporate structure.

After a long-drawn-out process, twelve months to be precise, which deeply affected my mental health and wellbeing, there was sadly no consideration for me. A deeply humiliating, intimidating, and fearful process, where I was told not to come to work, or enter the workplace unless to attend hearings. Unsupported, with any HR presence representing the corporate not the person, I was left alone and isolated to try to secure a new position somewhere else within that structure; as if this position I was now in was entirely my own fault. It was a token meaningless gesture, and it was deeply humiliating. During this time, I was dissociated with altogether. Colleagues were told not to contact me and were informed that I had an illness.

A process where, despite it being upheld, the code of conduct had been broken, and not by me, I was made to feel like the perpetrator of a great crime. I would like to say that I received some form of justice but that would be grossly incorrect. For in my diminishment, my poor mental health, and the immense fear, which was compounded further by the treatment I was receiving for standing up and challenging the structures and systems that ruled, after twelve months of stress and uncertainty I was presented with what felt like my only option. In my perceived need for a basic forwarding reference so that I could work again, and to continue to afford the roof over mine and my family's head, I did the worse thing possible. I sold my voice, a basic human right and in doing so, I diminished my Self further. Silenced by a piece of paper that I signed at the lowest point of my own mental wellbeing, like a blanket of fear for me to stay forever frozen within.

Some eight years later in pursuit of my own identification, of finding my Self, and in the process of connecting with my purpose and writing this book, I am saddened to see that I was afraid to speak whilst I was in it, and I am still afraid to speak now I am out of it. However, now with awareness, I see how by remaining silent, by not sharing ALL of my story, I remain frozen in my blanket of fear, shackled to these outdated concepts of structure and systems that control and do not serve anyone. Concepts that I ask you, in your own leadership, to consider for change.

If I remain in fear, I cannot fulfil my purpose to assist others with finding their true sense of Self so they can consider and create change within their leadership. This fear-based energy that is now the norm for the world we live in must be eradicated, it must be explored and discussed. My own experiences must be eradicated in the workplace, and so I choose, through sharing all my story, to face the fear. I owe that to my Self, and to all others who may resonate with my experiences, who feel at dis-ease and that seek a different way of leadership.

CONVERSATIONS WITH MY SOUL

It is indeed a sad story because these corporate structures sit blinded by the light of their own perceived power, unconscious to the disregard of the people, the power of the people and unconscious to how their own style of leadership not only diminishes others but also diminishes their own selves.

How can anyone reach the pinnacle of their potential, live a joyful and purposeful life, when they exploit and abuse others? They have no power, and their outdated structures and systems will crumble in these changing times, this leadership cannot be sustained.

As I have unfolded and encompassed my past into my present within these pages, I understand that every situation, every art of experience, has led me to my own connection to my authentic Self. And this is what I want you to find. By offering to you a new way of leadership in the next chapter, I hope to sow the seeds of considerations for change that will enable you to promote a healthier way of leadership that places people before profit.

Maybe you can also start to consider whether you are accepting the unacceptable in your leadership and workplace.

Take the time to consider before reading on.

CHAPTER 11

Concepts for Consideration for Change

FOR THE PAST 18 months or so, I have felt what I can only best describe to you as a deep sense of yearning to become all that I can be. Although my life is now serene, I am no longer in pain and at dis-ease with my Self I have felt a strong impulse to explore and step into my own potential. An innate knowing within that I need to try to create a difference in the workplace. I have a desire to bring balance into the workplace through introducing concepts for change to alleviate the pain and dis-ease these structures often manifest. We need to bring forth new leadership structures and systems, a more considered and conscious approach by balancing today's mascu-

line power-based structures with feminine power.

Once you have considered the Five Facets of
the Self, once you have identified, actualised,
and created change within your Self, you can
then start to consider change in your business
and leadership. The concepts of change I share
in this chapter are the foundation level for the
change that is needed to create a new mode of
conscious leadership.

CONVERSATIONS WITH MY SOUL

*The fact is that these four core concepts will have to
be implemented in order to survive, for the new way
is surging and pushing forward. It requires a consideration of structure, roles, responsibility, and recommendation.*

In my own consideration of my Self, I had a
realisation that I do not want to stay in the tradi-
tional female role of staying at home and raising
a family. Nor do I want to return to the current
corporate world for all the reasons I have shared
with you.

Nor do I simply want to combine the two to
prove that 'women can have it all' because as I

have experienced and now fully considered, the way it is at the moment, they cannot. In order to be successful in these structures, most woman who are trying to balance career and mother-hood 'having the best of both worlds, having it all' are indeed striving, they are in fact doing it all and not having it all. Most are out of balance on this elusive search for a work/life balance and are very much disconnected from their own sense of Self, their feminine power, because this is not found in today's workplace systems and structures. It is not even seen, and it is not known that it is needed and as such, as I have ex-perienced, it is not supported.

Women cannot actualise into their true po-tential in these masculine power-based struc-tures and systems and so leadership remains unbalanced. The barrier must be lifted. As you have read in my story I have struggled and strived and could not fulfil my own potential. Upon consideration I understand that the pri-mary reason I felt so at dis-ease with myself, was largely due to the masculine concepts of success and power that define leadership in the work-place and the world today. Woman have lost their own power and leadership is unbalanced. Feminine leadership is intuitive, it is creative, it is thoughtful, caring, compassion and it is CON-SIDERATE.

I do not wish to enter into a gender struggle here. I am not saying that the masculine leadership of logical, strategic, action planned approach is wrong or that masculine leadership is not considered. What I am saying is that it needs to be balanced, and that this balance is achieved through a rising consciousness which is an individual responsibility. It starts with every individual leader through an identification of the Self first. Through this process you connect to your own values, ethics, ethos, and priorities. You find balance in your Self, by bringing the feminine energy (Yin) into the masculine (Yang) that exists in us all, you come into unity. When you have unity in your Self, you eliminate the stress, the struggle, and the striving because you eradicate the fear that creates the control that you are in and the control that you are. Then, secondly you create balance in your business leadership, through building a strong and balanced foundation constructed upon the considerations for change that enable the systems and structures to support and consider all people. Coming into unity in this way naturally enables and supports the feminine aspects of leadership. There needs to be a recognition that there is a difference, not a right or a wrong way and that both masculine and feminine leadership attributes are needed.

Through the considerations for change, where you look at your structures and systems that do not support or rise the feminine and by conceptualising and consolidating the change, you bring a balanced way of leadership. A way that allows the wheel of your company structure to turn. By considering the concepts I present that allow every person within that structure to be themselves, you automatically and organically bring your systems and structures into balance. Balance is the desired state. When we bring all structures and systems that govern and lead into balance, we bring everything into balance, people, and planet. This needs to be understood, for our capacity to be productive as human beings is not in the way that we are currently functioning.

This is not a feminist approach. As I highlighted in the introduction, I am referring to feminine leadership attributes. Let me share an example of a feminine leadership attribute that I once perceived for myself as a shortcoming, a failing. This was to take time to pause, to connect and listen to my own intuition, to listen to all, to think and to consider before making a decision that would have a significant impact on people and sometimes the planet. In the corporate structures I experienced, this was misinterpreted as an inability to be decisive and perceived as a failure to make a quick decision. I would struggle to be heard if I could not logically articulate my reasons in a very analytical and logical way. Part of my decision process was coming from my intuition, and as such it was based on a feeling. If I used the expression 'I feel' this was regarded as being 'wishy washy', invalid and not worthy of being heard.

In a masculine way of work, it is seen as a highly regarded CV worthy accolade to be a 'fast decision maker' and in some cases, in the leadership that I experienced, of deciding alone and without the need for consulting all of your team. There was little consideration of the impact as you seek your own personal recognition for achieving this desired leadership and CV worthy skill. It doesn't really matter about the consequences of that decision because if it suits, you can make the outcome someone else's responsibility. This fast-paced approach makes no sense to me, as if speed of decision, 'being a fast decision maker', is more important than making the right decision through giving yourself time and space to consider.

As I have already shared, it is in the pause, the stillness, that success is found. In my own pause and consideration, I see that this was not a shortcoming or a failure on my part, this was one of my feminine attributes that I intuitively used in my leadership, which contributed greatly to the successful outcomes I delivered. The feminine way is considerate, it is reflective, it is collective, and it is supportive, it uses inner intuition and knowing. It has been lost many centuries ago because the female intuition has been feared not revered, and now today because systems and structures do not support these leadership attributes; women in these roles have learned the masculine way. I know this because I was wholly unauthentically masculine in my leadership approach at the end of my career. I became highly organised, operational, analytical, logical but without kindness, compassion, or time for consideration of myself or another. Whilst this approach is highly effective when the focus is all profit-based and there is a predictable outcome, people need to come before profit, and these are unpredictable times; the workplace will not be the same again. Balance is needed in leadership and in the systems and structures that lead and govern it. It is this balance that is the art of being.

CONVERSATIONS WITH MY SOUL

Therefore, to bring it into balance, the feminine aspect and attributes within your structure must be considered. For the current structure, in its inflexibility, its limitedness becomes a liability. A structure is meant to be solid in its foundation, a liability is not a solid structure. A liability is a systemised expectation, and a systemised expectation cannot present itself as a structure. Therefore, what I ask you to consider is what expectations are placed upon you that creates an unsecure system?

And as this is considered, you then, in your leadership, consider your company structure, your roles/responsibility, your reputation, your recommendation, people, purpose, productivity and profit. You consider the new and the old, you consider the change in your new way. You give yourself time to think and to find the solutions. You do not seek outwards, but you seek inner guidance. This is the art of being.

It is then to consider whether you are then overloaded, overwhelmed, or overworked. Seldom are you overjoyed. Seldom are you in the laughter and the lightness of your personality that sparks the insight to be more creative. To be more productive from your ability to flow, loving life and the art of conversation, this has long gone. Seldom has one considered the care and consideration to take time to reflect, to consider health and wellbeing and whether your thoughts stress you or support you. If for anybody the garbage is never taken out, if the earth in its seasonal cycles did not decay then it becomes overloaded.

When overloaded, the new cannot properly be birthed, you are forever trying to clean up a mess where the new cannot grow properly. To stop and think about old ways that do not work allows the considerations for the new, your own art of being, to be more birthed, to be more in productive fruition. In si-

lence and stillness, the more feminine attributes to leadership, you have that time to consider it. If you are always responding, solving, sorting, this consideration process does not have the same level of delivery because the answers you will be presented with will be external to your inner intelligence. As you allow the intelligence that has come through these 'time out' considerations, there becomes a completion of the change, the decay of the old, the birth of the new.

When you really consider your Self there is an inner guidance system within you, an inner guidance system that gives you the answers and this begins to eliminate the stress, the struggle, and the striving. These three S's separate you from your essence.

As a new way dawns, a new way approaches. The blindfold is coming off to what has been. This is a wakeup call into awareness, acceptance, and action. Action is needed.

Our world is rapidly changing. It will change, and it will require a new way. These waves of change are here and for businesses to thrive in these changing times, I would like to present the four core Concepts for Consideration for Change:

1. Company
2. Community
3. Connection
4. Creation

Many companies do not have a community or a connection to people and in this way, they limit creation because people are not placed before production or profit. Therefore, the creation, by which I mean bringing out the true potential of the people, is limited or does not exist.

I do not dispute the fact that there are of course values in companies and there is customer care, but there are many shortcomings. There are many shortcomings to a company that has one aim, where success is profit driven. Where supply and demand are reached for like a robotic systematic structure that dehumanises a community, a connection, a sense of belonging, the ability to communicate and express creation, where people are actually deskilled.

Therefore, a company that works this way may be in profit, but it is also in deficit, for it lacks. This way of business as I have shared throughout this book, will be outmoded for the simple reason that whilst we are witnessing many financial changes, many structures being demanding through this pandemic, we are also seeing a rising of people wanting a deeper meaning to work, life, and leadership.

CONVERSATIONS WITH MY SOUL

COMPANY

The new way of leadership that I am asking you to consider places emphasis and the spotlight on the Company. When the Company can speak and express their ethos, ethics, and values they will attract the right people, with the right personality, with the right level of respect that will reach their potential. Companies in their social responsibility (which will no longer be about giving a small amount and thinking this will suffice, this will not suffice), they will need to have emotion. They will need to feel a sense of duty, a sense of responsibility for those less fortunate and to integrate themselves into understanding something, knowing something, and giving back to something.

In the new way there is an honour to people, an honour to give back to the community, and to a wider broader economy. Community means commitment to a shared honour, a shared value, a shared responsibility, where everyone's role is respected, not above, not below, where the triangle of hierarchy can turn itself around.

This level of community gives commitment, it gives attributes, it unleashes the attributes of humanity on a wider scale where companies do not have a high turnover of staff, or struggle or strife, nor sickness or stress, for everything is interlinked and inter-placed.

COMMUNITY

There is little or no sense of community in a company where the depth of the meaning is on productivity and profit, it limits itself in this way. I wish to give you a definition of community for you to consider, because when it is worked with and implemented and structured in a way which defines its meaning, there is more capacity to be unlimited through understanding a human dynamic.

Community means to come into unity with the company, together where all pieces make the whole, where all pieces are seen as equally important, a person-centred community. Therefore, when a company responds more as a community, and whilst there are boundaries and lines of accountability, I am not disputing this, it is of course important to understand where one's role and responsibilities start and end. What I am saying is, when you come into a sense of connectiveness and togetherness, the hierarchy crumbles.

Where all pieces of the whole are needed to create an outcome, an objective. Where all people are seen as important, with an important role, an important re-

sponsibility, an important part. Therefore, if you have a community, there is little exploitation. In our current workplace of pick up and run, of fast-track, getting and receiving, of demand and desire, to fulfil an unsatisfied spirit, people have learned to exploit. Exploitation has no place in a new way of leadership, the new paradigm of business dynamics that I am asking you to consider.

Even if you are a sole trader, there must still be a community because the rising of any business is no longer about forging forward on your own or forging forward over another. If you do, then you are not in the essence of company, you are in the essence of competition and there is no compassion or kindness, the feminine energy of leadership.

For smaller businesses, a community really is a collaboration of understanding that it will take several people to support, several people to help, to give and to give without getting, to have no agenda. Therefore, smaller businesses must look at who will kindly support them, who would promote them, who would hold out a hand of help, freely given, where the rewards of giving are huge, where the reward is acknowledged, where your helpers are acknowledged, and a give back is given. This is not about get and take and use and abuse. This is a rising of one's energy through truly desiring to see another be successful. It is the source of the human spirit and yet in our human form on a wider level of humanity, we have been too fearful *to give, too frightened to feel the senses of our own insecurity, and to look at another's success without jealously.*

CONNECTION

Being in unity instantly gives a connection, when there is a connection, there is interest. There is an ability to respond, there is innovation, inspiration, aspiration. Connection means you begin to feel a sense of belonging, you feel proud of the company's ethos, values, and ethics, of how they work, what they are about.

You have a belonging. You have a connection that connects you from your Soul where you can connect, communicate, express, be a wider part of something, a place where you can unleash your potential. When these attributes are around there is a natural creation, there is more progression, more spontaneous ideas, more productivity, more creativity, more potential through the human spirit being extended and set free to be. Free from the constraints of the way that should be, where a diminishment of the Self is no longer. A new way forward allows the Self to excel.

Take the emphasis off production and profit and put it onto yourself and your leadership. When you understand that this has an energy, an inspiration, an aspiration, an innovation, taking flight is easier, because your body senses the desires and passion that is needed, like the fuel that drives a car, the fuel that takes a plane in the air and propels it. This is what I am speaking to you about. Therefore, it is in the introspection of the Self that allows a business to take off, to truly get into the core desire.

CREATION

Creation comes from working in connection and collaboration with others, it comes from community and a sense of oneness, of company. When the structure is aligned with the first three Concepts for Considerations for Change, this fourth consideration of creation, is a natural outcome.

Creation is to construct an even greater sense of Self in life and leadership through balance, through giving birth to your own persona, your own personality, your own presence. Being very aligned with what is right for that person by giving themselves permission to be, permission to do, permission to create, but most of all to do it in their unique way, accelerates health and wealth.

If the systems and structure promote and support everyone's unique special purpose, then creation becomes unlimited. If the systems and structures do not control, but promote equality and free expression, where the energy is no longer fear-based, there is no need to compete and compare yourself or to control and exploit others, then creation becomes unlimited. When everyone's contribution is valued the same, when reward is shared, when you are connected to your Self and have considered these concepts, conceptualised, and implemented them, there will be a sense of unity.

I invite you to just take a moment to imagine the collective creation that would result through the implementation of these four core concepts. Consider if you worked in this way, what would your company look like? The energy wasted on control and fear through a loss of the Self, through systems and structures that do not support or serve anyone, that result in the struggling, striving, and stressing, could be focused on these concepts for change and solutions to the real issues facing humanity could be sought.

This is why these concepts have been channelled. This is why you are being asked to consider and identify with your Self, to stop being unconscious in your leadership, to connect to a greater consciousness through your own inner intelligence that knows how to be. This knowing is within each of us, it has been lost under many layers of misplaced values, behaviours, thought processes and outdated concepts that do not serve the human spirit.

As you build on your definition of these four core concepts and understand that the building of this community is connection. Where every piece fits into the whole and every piece is honoured and respected and therefore a sense of belonging, a sense of honour, a sense of mutual support, sharing, rises into more. Where rewards are shared, where creation is honoured, where you are continually considering how can you support another's potential and how can you give back. Where everyone's desire and passion to work with their purpose and potential is brought into creation, you maximise, with respect, every person's unique individual skill.

In this respect, USP is no longer a unique selling point where it all becomes about sales and profit. It is about the special potential within your uniqueness and when you begin to unleash and open this you rise higher. These are the contributing four factors that need to be figured out, starting with your own identification, through the Five Facets of the Self.

These four core concepts that I have presented to you as considerations for change, are often overlooked, under acknowledged or not acknowledged at all and so this is a different perspective to leadership.

CONVERSATIONS WITH MY SOUL

Externally people will want a sense of belonging, they will be prepared to invest and to pay more for those company's products and services that honour the ways of humanity. They will want to be employed by those who give terms and conditions that have a respect for each person's life and leadership. This is a new way that leads to a natural way of PR, a natural way of presentation, a natural way of marketing. These will be based on emotion, need, and on the depth of character to care for another. Marketing is about relationships, it is all about people coming together to collaborate in community, it is all about the concepts of change, it is all about considering.

Success is no longer singular and cannot survive. By helping each other, giving without an agenda, the crumbling of hierarchy will happen and therefore it is in your company that you create community, it is in collaboration, it is in connection that one creates.

If you haven't yet taken time to consider the Five Facets of the Self, I invite you to take a pause and to do this, let's recap upon those:

1. Do you know your own values and beliefs?

2. Do you know how you define success and happiness?
3. Do you know what brings you fulfilment?
4. Do you know what your priority is in life or leadership?
5. Do you know how you wish to relate to yourself and to others?

Once you have considered and identified with your true Self, you can consider these concepts for change and the words which I have shared in this chapter.

Please do not rush as these words speak of a new way, a different way of being in life and leadership and these may be concepts that are very unfamiliar to you, depending upon where you are in your own journey, of self-identification and actualisation. Therefore, do not stress, struggle, or strive to understand, I am just inviting you to gently consider.

CHAPTER 12

New Ways of Leadership

WHILST I HAVE SHARED with you all that I intended to for your own gentle consideration, for the purpose of conclusion I would like to offer to you some further extracts of channelled wisdom that speak of this new dimensional mode of leadership. They encompass why I have written this book and why I am asking you to consider this change in your own leadership.

CONVERSATIONS WITH MY SOUL

People have been treated as if they are nothing, input, output, throughput, a flow and let go of people, this is not a sustainable way. When you bring out someone's potential, when you honour them through respect and loyalty and commitment, where they are rewarded, where they are given a share of their hard work, there is a sense of belonging that creates a community, a connection that is unbreakable. When this happens, it ignites the senses, people begin to feel what is important and what is a priority.

Companies will have to show that they are worthy and can be trusted to have good solid collaborations/relationships. There can be no more divide, for in division there is no understanding, there is no relating.

Companies will have to offer incentives and they will have to honour their values. The market forces we are now seeing will force them to respect their people and to bring out their potential. This is the only way to ensure sustainable productivity and profit, by looking after their people in a way that there is not a consistent turnover of staff.

Through consideration comes change in the structures and systems to provide more opportunities, more profit share, more training, more understanding of all the intelligences - emotional, mindful, and physical, recognition of stress, of strain, of work/life balance. As I see it, reviewing the history of dark ages, the early industrial revolution, of poor working conditions, long hours, and poor pay, and yet hundreds of years, centuries on... how much difference do you see?

Understanding roles and responsibilities is the success of the whole, supporting is the success of the whole. True leadership is not a separation from staff, but it is supporting them. Leaders are the scaffolding that holds it all up and so this is a 360-degree turnaround. Those at the top are often very separated from a deep sense of Self, a sense of survival, a sense of security, a sense of serenity, and a sense of sustainability. They are too scared to admit they sense nothing.

In order for companies at a larger level to thrive, they will have to change. Everything will change. No longer can people be used and abused as this is diminishment of their psychology.

Let's consider productivity. Productivity is the person; a person is productive. Without a person unless you are using a machine, there is no productivity. Therefore, in your leadership role you are an investor in productivity, an investor in potential, and an investor in the person. You are an investor in the systems and structures that create a sense of belonging to a company, rather like a family. In a functioning family the person is nourished, supported, cared for, guided, and educated. A functioning family provides the ingredients that allows the person to excel. Sadly, in these dysfunctional times this is lacking in many family environments, and it has been absolutely shattered and dismantled in work corporations and companies. In a world that is going online, in a world that is breeding entrepreneurs and self-employment there will be a need for company leaders to ensure productivity for survival.

In the current climate of complete uncertainty, people will have to work together, give together, and share together. The squeeze of productivity to get as much out of someone, like squeezing the last piece of a tube regardless of how painful, exhausting, stressful that is, the squeeze to create productivity and profit will no longer sustain. A thriving business or company will have to understand their values, their relationships, their ethics, their ethos, their collaborations, and their community. They will have to come together to join productivity in certain circumstances. They will have to become investors in their community, invest in the potential of people who share a return. A psychology of consistently making more is madness. If there is a constant squeeze in this way, they will find they are in an outdated and outmoded way of thinking.

A company's certainty about their productivity lies in the heart of how they relate. It begins with an education for senior leaders to be able to relate better to themselves, for no external relationship can come until this relationship is absolutely and utterly explored.

An unhappy workforce is an unproductive workforce which is unsustainable and not long lived. There is no promotion of potential in an environment where there is a high level of toxic sickness, staff turnover and general dis-ease. When someone is inspired by their own purpose and productivity then profit is a natural and actual response. When someone can see their Self, their potential, their power, and their passion then profit is a natural and actual response. When a philosophy is filtered through a company (and each company must find their personal philosophy), through people focused leadership and productivity - profit will come.

Leaders who invest in this approach to productivity, who invest in their people, in themselves, in their company values, ethos and mission statement, (that must all be adhered to), who create ways that enables every individual to explore their higher purpose and their potential, will birth more productivity and profit.

Therefore, exploitation is a limitation, it is a limitation to the human potential. It is a limitation to human productivity and to human profit. Exploitation diminishes the emotions, it diminishes innovation, inspiration, and aspiration. Where the potential of anyone is simply squashed it is denied, it is diminished and then the human spirit becomes a robotic machine devoid of a sense of perception that ignites the potential within.

This is what my spirit felt when I was in the corporate machine, and this is what I want to change through offering to you, in your leadership, these concepts for change for your consideration.

I can understand that these concepts for change that I ask you to consider within your leadership may seem counterintuitive. I am asking you to invest in an approach to productivity and profit that is different. It may seem counterproductive, particularly if you are in profit, but if you consider these changes this will enable you to build a strong foundation, which will allow you to flourish in financial flow and financial freedom.

This is a long haul not a short-term quick fix as change is created over a longer, sustainable period. By asking you to see differently, to think differently, to sense differently, to perceive differently and to be different is a complete turnaround of identification on every level. It will take time, but you will reap the benefits of this new way of leadership, as will the people you lead.

CONVERSATIONS WITH MY SOUL

*When you eliminate the pain of being stressed, unful-
filled, in conflict or in crisis either with the company
or your Self, if you alleviate a sense of unhappiness
and disease then you elevate the person. If the human
spirit is elevated, your emotion and mind allow the
creation of aspiration, innovation, and inspiration.
The igniting of that emotion brings forth someone's
passion and desire to be in their purpose, to be in their
potential, and to be productive. When a human being
is inspired to be productive, they become profitable,
not through exploitation, not through the stressors,
but through elevation into the evolution of their potential. Through an ability to relate to themselves, to
relate to the company, to relate to the position and to
relate to the people through being an investor in these
concepts for change.*

*Eradication is the word, alleviate. Then it is to elevate,
evolve into company values of connection, community, and creation where opportunities for all are
shared. Initiatives and incentives, added bonuses,
team building, the acknowledgement of basic human
needs not to survive but to thrive. For beyond thriving
is the activation of potential, it means beyond emotional and physical safety. It is all in the ability to
relate to the Self and the company and then to a wider
workforce. This is the difference between sink or*

swim for all people where the levels of hierarchy cannot sustain their definition. For in order to come into these concepts of change, the definable structure of hierarchy must mingle in order to know each other, understand each other, discover each other. No more a case of never the twain shall meet, there must be a different way to relate.

I know from my own experiences in leadership that there is much pain in the workplace. I felt this at an extreme level and felt the loss of potential, through the loss of being able to relate in the way this channelled message highlights. My experiences that I have shared with you must be erased if certainty in any company is to survive. Many of you are in leadership roles, like I was for many years, within a corporate culture that has manufactured your thoughts and your feelings, beliefs and your definitions and concepts. You may be feeling at dis-ease in many aspects of life. Unconscious of how you are being, of where your sense of being is, your behaviour, your thoughts, your programmes, your conditioning and the control through which you have absorbed concepts that are old and worn out, which separate you from your being. Culture is only a concept of mind. I am asking you to consider a different culture by exploring these concepts for change that allows the individual to be present, to be explored, and to be identified.

As these considerations are implemented into a concept, a company or corporate concept, and you ground it in everything, these considerations allow an emergence of certainty in these uncertain times. Certainty of stability and of building a strong foundation through being considerate.

CONVERSATIONS WITH MY SOUL

The current culture is a concept that has no concept of its destruction. These considerations for change are how you construct. The consideration in these uncertain times can no longer be on a profit only driven approach, it is not sustainable and will not give any corporation or company certainty.

A consideration is to be considerate. To consider another is to change.

When you seek a new sense of Self, the business appears, the change in the company appears. It is a consciousness that ignites your own inner intellectual force. This is emergence, it is the birthing of a new way, a new you, a new dawn, a new paradigm. You are leaving behind in this paradigm the pain, the dis-ease, the illness, the toxicity, and the sickness of separating from a sense of being that has no concept, because your being is rarely considered.

I shall pause for a moment for this is new and will need to be considered. Take stock of what you have read and so how much of this applies to your life? How can you change as a leader?

It takes a brave person to actualise these changes and to lead differently. I invite you to consider if you are ready to explore your own sense of Self, to disengage with outdated concepts and emerge in a new way of leadership? It is this kind of leader that is needed to deliver a new dimensional mode of conscious leadership. This kind of leader is ready to step out, is ready to speak, to express, is ready to face themselves and their fear. This kind of leader wants to discover and understand the needs of their team, understand the potential and the productivity of people.

It is a leadership that works with kindness and consideration through a consciousness connection to themselves and others.

These times of change are here.

I invite you to consider.

CHAPTER 13

What's Next?

FROM MY LIFE EXPERIENCES that I have shared, my own considerations, and through the channelled wisdom I have received, that has led to my own identification of the Self, I found myself with a unique set of principles designed to serve others in business leadership. It is from these that I have set up my company, The Art of *Being* in Business. The foundations of which are deeply rooted in the ancient principles of leadership and the concepts for change I present to you for consideration in this book.

Before I put down my pen and finish this book, I would like to invite you to consider the following questions:

- Despite being 'successful' do you feel at dis-ease? Do you feel stressed, anxious, unhappy, or even depressed?
- Do you feel unauthentic in your leadership role, feeling pressure to think, feel and behave a certain way that just doesn't feel aligned to your own values, morals, ethics, or persona?
- Do you suffer from the 'imposter syndrome' and feel unworthy of or not good enough for your success or leadership?
- Do you feel limited in your potential, feeling stuck and unfulfilled despite giving it your all?
- Do you feel a desire to rediscover your own unique talents and gifts and find your true, deep, and meaningful purpose in business?
- Do you find yourself over giving and over doing, feeling burnt out by the demands of your leadership and feel out of balance with work and life?
- Maybe you just feel different in your leadership, that you don't quite fit the mould?
- Maybe you want to create change in the workplace yet feel overwhelmed, confused, and powerless to make a difference?

If you answer yes to any of the questions and would like to find out more about how I could work with you, I would be delighted to connect with you. Through my programmes I will guide and support you through a process that will create the change you seek in your Self and your leadership. A process I refer to as the Navigation of the Self. Why?

Because I have learned that:

- It is in the Self that success lies, in your ability to see who you are, what you are and where you want to go.
- That your inner intelligence holds all the answers that you seek.
- Before you can create change in your leadership or business, you must first create change in your Self.

The Navigation of the Self is a 5-step process that forms the foundation of all my programmes. Through this process you will build your own bespoke personal foundation from which to thrive. Incorporating the Five Facets of the Self, I will guide you through your own identification, actualisation, consideration, consolidation, and emergence in a completely new way.

In this process you will start to release from the ego and the mind, for these separate you from yourself, from others, from purpose, from the planet and from the infinite, the five major relationships that allow you to excel.

With this book and my work, I invite you to consider concepts for a new psychology of leadership. A way of leadership that I would love to be the height of fashion by the end of the decade - a way of leadership that will become 'the new normal'.

Thank you for taking a pause and finding time to read this book. Perhaps this is your calling to consider?

From one open heart to another,

Esther x

About the Author

ESTHER WALKER HAS WORKED within leadership roles within large global corporations for over 20 years, 8 years ago after reaching her definition of 'success' she walked away from this path. Esther shares a very honest and open account of her experiences within these roles that led her to consider a different way of leadership, and to write this book. She presents considerations for change for a way of leadership that is far removed from her experiences of leadership, within masculine power-based corporate structures. She shares her story of how striving for a definition of success, that she had never really considered for herself, of how living disconnected and without awareness of her true identity, her spirit, and her purpose, eventually led her to seek a very different path.

An unusual path, that has taken her on a journey that she refers to as a Navigation of the Self. A journey that Esther now guides others through. During her own reflection, Esther has sought her own definition of success which is to find and work with her own meaningful purpose.

During this period of her own reflection and consideration, Esther has experienced a most uncommon dialogue through channelled wisdom that relates directly to her experiences within the workplace. An extraordinary dialogue she refers to as 'Conversations with my Soul'.

Esther's *why* for writing this book is twofold. Firstly, she desires for others who may relate to her story, who are struggling and striving, feeling in pain or at dis-ease within their leadership roles, to know that they are not alone and that there is hope, because there is a different way.

Secondly, the channelled wisdom in this book was gifted to Esther and she gifts it to you with the highest hope that its root of delivery is honoured and that this wisdom is considered. It is Esther's purpose and heartfelt wish that with this book she will connect with those leaders that are ready to consider and consolidate change.

Through the wisdom and teachings channelled to her, Esther has set up her company, The Art of *Being* in Business and is delighted to offer a number of programmes for business leaders.

If you would like to work more closely with Esther and would like more information, please visit Esther's website at:

www.theartofbeinginbusiness.co.uk.

CONVERSATIONS WITH MY SOUL

The mountain does not move,

those that seek the mountain come to it,

and in doing so the mountain shall share.

When the mountain shares,

all those around the mountain are ready to listen and receive.

Lightning Source UK Ltd.
Milton Keynes UK
UKHW021836201221
395980UK00004B/10